Teen Girl's Handbook

Book 2

FIND YOUR VOICE

SET BOUNDARIES, BUILD RESILIENCE

AND LIVE WITH PURPOSE

Teenskill Surge

Contents

A Note from the Author

H i, I'm Monika — the heart behind *Teen Girl's Handbook: Book 2.*

If you're holding this book, you're ready to go a little deeper—to explore purpose, boundaries, and resilience in a world that often feels confusing and loud. I wrote this companion volume as a guide for every girl learning to protect her peace, use her voice, and step confidently into her next chapter.

This book isn't about becoming someone new — it's about remembering who you already are. It's about uncovering your strength, your faith in yourself, and your ability to grow even when life feels uncertain.

My hope is that these pages remind you that your boundaries matter, your voice matters, and your growth matters — even when it's quiet or unseen. You don't need to rush your journey. You're allowed to take your time and trust that becoming takes patience.

Thank you for letting me walk alongside you through these words. Wherever you are in your story, I hope you'll keep choosing courage, kindness, and truth — the real foundations of confidence.

With gratitude and encouragement,
— **Monika**

For updates, encouragement, and new releases, scan the QR code below to follow **MM Legacy Publishing** on Facebook for helpful resources and upcoming books from both the **TeenSkill Surge** and **Graceful Growth** collections.

READER BONUS

Bonus #1 – Teen Girl's Handbook Companion

Access your free journal to start building confidence and calm today!

Scan the QR code to download your bonus guide.

Start exploring right away — it's yours to keep and enjoy.

Bonus #2 — Teen Girl's Handbook (Book 1)

Start where it all began!

Strengthen your confidence, manage stress, and build real friendships with the first book in the series. Every page helps you grow a little braver, calmer, and kinder to yourself.

Scan the QR code to download your copy!

Bonus #3 — Personal Finance Secrets for Teens and Young Adults

Get money-smart for the real world!

Discover 7 powerful hacks for saving, budgeting, and building lifelong financial freedom. Learn how to make your money work for you — not the other way around.

Scan the QR code to grab your guide!

Introduction

Y ou've already come a long way—through moments of doubt, stress, friendship shifts, and figuring out who you are in a world that often tells you who to be.

You may have joined me in *Book 1* and begun building confidence one small, honest step at a time. Or maybe this is your first time opening these pages—either way, you're in the right place.

This book is about what comes *after* learning to believe in yourself—what it means to **speak up, protect your peace, bounce back** when things get hard, and build a life that feels real, not performative.

Because here's the truth: **confidence isn't the finish line. It's the foundation.**

Once you know your worth, you can start shaping your world around it.

Maybe you've found your voice, but still struggle to use it when things get tense. Perhaps you're learning that setting boundaries doesn't mean pushing people away—it means keeping your energy safe. Or maybe you've been knocked down by change, rejection, or failure, and you're ready to rise again, stronger and clearer than before.

Wherever you are, this book is here to help you find your footing—to help you grow from the inside out.

***

We'll talk about things no one teaches in class but everyone needs to know:

- How to speak up with confidence—even when your voice shakes.

- How to say "no" without guilt and protect your time, peace, and priorities.

- How to build resilience when life feels unfair or overwhelming.

- How to live with purpose—making choices that reflect your values, not just expectations.

- How to understand yourself deeply, so that you can lead with empathy and strength.

- How to use your voice to create impact—in your friendships, school, and community.

You'll read stories from real teens learning to navigate friendships, identity, boundaries, and burnout—people who discovered that strength isn't about staying unbreakable. It's about learning how to bend without losing yourself.

And just like before, there's no judgment here. No fake perfection. No pretending that growth always feels good. It's messy sometimes—but it's also where confidence turns into courage.

This book isn't about becoming someone new. It's about coming home to yourself. The part of you that already knows when something feels wrong, when a boundary needs to be drawn, when it's time to rest, or when it's time to leap.

You'll find reflection prompts, real stories, and simple tools to help you move through challenging moments and create the kind of calm strength that lasts. You'll also find reminders that it's okay not to have all the answers yet—growth takes time, and purpose unfolds one small choice at a time.

By the end, I hope you'll see that your voice matters. Your boundaries matter. Your dreams, even the quiet ones, matter. You don't have to prove your worth—you have to live it.

Take a deep breath. You're ready.

This is your time to stand tall, speak up, and live like the main character of your own story—on your terms, in your power, with your heart wide open.

Let's begin.

Chapter 1

Real Talk on Mental Health

From Anxiety to Asking for Help

P icture this: you're sitting in class before a quiz. Your heart's racing, your palms are sweaty, and your stomach feels like it's tied in knots. Your teacher calls on you, and for a second, you feel totally exposed. Even after the quiz is over, your mind keeps spinning while everyone else seems fine.

That's not just nerves. For many girls, that's anxiety—and it's a lot more common than you might think. You're not alone in this.

***

ANXIETY IN OVERDRIVE — WHEN IT'S MORE THAN JUST STRESS

Stress happens to everyone. You get nervous before a big game, a performance, or meeting new people. Usually, it fades once the moment passes.

Anxiety is different. It lingers. It can sneak in even when there's no real reason, making your body and mind feel on high alert all the time. It could be triggered by school, relationships, or even just the thought of the future.

It might look like:

- a racing heart or tight chest

- an upset stomach or shaky hands

- endless *"what if"* thoughts that won't turn off.

Sometimes, anxiety makes you avoid things you used to enjoy. You might skip a party, say no to a sleepover, or stay home where it feels safe. At night, your brain replays every conversation, and by morning, you're already tired.

If your mind feels like it's always running and your body never gets a break, that's not *"just stress."* It's a sign that something deeper is happening. But remember, seeking help is a sign of strength, not weakness. You have the power to take control of your mental health.

And here's the truth: anxiety isn't weakness or drama. It's a real mental health challenge that affects millions of teens—top students, athletes, introverts, extroverts, everyone. It's okay to not be okay sometimes.

Experts, including the Child Mind Institute, say anxiety disorders are among the most common issues teens face today. Your brain isn't broken—it's doing its job, just a little too well. It's trying to protect you, but the alarm system, which is responsible for your fight or flight response, has become too sensitive, triggering anxiety even when there's no real threat.

***

Real Stories, Real Struggles

Anxiety doesn't always show up as panic attacks. Sometimes it hides behind perfect grades, fake smiles, or constant "I'm fine."

One girl told me she used to fake being sick before sleepovers because she was scared of having a panic attack in front of others. She thought she was "too sensitive" until a teacher noticed and checked in. That small talk opened the door for her to get help—and things slowly got easier.

Another girl quit trying out for clubs she loved because anxiety convinced her she'd embarrass herself. She kept saying, *"Maybe next year,"* until she realized she wasn't lazy—she was scared. Recognizing that fear for what it was helped her take the first step toward getting support.

These stories aren't rare—they're just usually hidden behind smiles and silence.

***

Why It's Not "All in Your Head"

When people don't understand anxiety, they sometimes say things like "Just calm down," "Stop overthinking," or "You're fine." But anxiety isn't a switch you can flip off—it's your brain trying to protect you from things it *thinks* are dangerous, even when you're actually safe. It's a normal, human response.

That racing heartbeat? The sweaty palms? The shaky hands? They're not signs of weakness. They're proof that your body is reacting to fear signals your brain is sending out too often.

Experts from the Child Mind Institute explain that anxiety disorders are among the most common challenges teens face today. You're not alone in this. What you're feeling isn't rare—it's human. You're not overreacting. You're experiencing something real that deserves understanding, not judgment.

Your brain isn't broken—it's just overprotective. It's like having an overactive security system that sounds the alarm even when there's no danger. And just like any system, it can be trained to calm down again.

With time, awareness, and the right tools—like deep breathing, therapy, journaling, or reaching out for help—you can teach your brain that you're safe.

Anxiety doesn't define you. It's something you *experience*, not something you *are*. You are not your anxiety. You are so much more.

And every time you take a step to care for your mental health, you're proving to yourself that strength and sensitivity can coexist beautifully.

***

Self-Check: Is It More Than Stress?

Ask yourself honestly:

- **How often do I feel anxious**—every day, a few times a week, or only before significant events?

- **Do I get physical symptoms** (like racing heart, nausea, or sweating) even when nothing stressful is happening?

- **Do I avoid certain people, places, or activities** because of fear or worry?

- **Has my sleep changed**—trouble falling asleep, waking up anxious, or never feeling rested?

- **Do I feel restless or unable to relax** most of the time?

- **Are my worries hard to control**, even when others tell me "there's nothing to worry about"?

- **Have I ever had a panic attack**—sudden, intense fear with physical symptoms?

- **Is anxiety getting in the way** of school, friendships, or things I care about?

If several of these sound familiar—or if this feels like most days—it's worth getting support. You don't have to wait until things feel "bad enough."

***

What's Actually Happening Inside You

When you're anxious, your body releases stress hormones like adrenaline and cortisol. They're the same chemicals that help you run from danger. The problem? Your brain can trigger them even when there *isn't* danger—like before a quiz or a text reply that's taking too long.

That's why you can't just "think your way out" of anxiety. Your mind and body are connected, so real healing usually takes both mental and physical tools: breathing, movement, rest, and support.

It's not weakness—it's biology.

***

Breaking the Silence

Because of stigma, talking about anxiety can feel risky. But remember, asking for help doesn't mean giving up—it means taking your power back. It's okay to ask for help, just like you would if you sprained your ankle. Mental health deserves the same care.

Try starting small. You can say something like:

"I've been feeling really anxious lately, and it's starting to get in the way of school and friends."

or

"I think I need to talk to someone about how anxious I've been feeling."

You don't have to have all the words. You need to open the door.

If the first person you talk to doesn't get it, try another—like a teacher, school counselor, parent, coach, aunt, pastor, or even a helpline. There's always someone willing to listen; sometimes it just takes a few tries to find the right one. But remember, once you find the proper support, things can start to get better.

***

Signs You Deserve Support (Spoiler: You Do)

It's time to reach out if:
- Anxiety is stealing your joy or making you avoid life.
- You're tired of feeling "on edge" every day.
- You've stopped doing things you love because of fear.
- You feel hopeless or think it will never change.

Getting help isn't about labeling yourself—it's about getting tools to manage what's already happening.

Support can look different for everyone:

- talking with a counselor or therapist

- learning grounding techniques or mindfulness

- journaling or creative outlets like art and music

- trying exercise, relaxation, or new sleep routines

- getting professional help, including medication if needed.

You don't have to face this alone or "fix it" on your own. There are people trained to help you breathe again, think clearly, and find peace.

***

A Message You Might Need to Hear

> You are not broken.
> You are not too much.
> You are not dramatic.

You're dealing with something real, and it's okay to ask for help before you hit your breaking point.

The same strength you use to get through anxiety every day is the same strength that will help you get through healing.

You deserve relief—not just survival.

Reflection Prompt: My Anxiety Reality Check

Write or think about:

- What situations trigger my anxiety most often?

- What do I usually do to cope—and does it help?

- Who could I talk to if I needed support today?

- What's one thing I wish people understood about how anxiety feels for me?

You don't have to fix it all at once. Awareness itself is a form of progress.

***

One Last Thought

Anxiety that takes up space in your mind, body, or daily life isn't something to ignore. It's not a flaw—it's a signal.

When your body is whispering "I'm not okay," the kindest thing you can do is listen.

Reaching out for help doesn't make you weak—it makes you wise enough to care for yourself.

You are never alone in this. And the first step—naming it—is already brave.

***

DEPRESSION ISN'T DRAMA — WHAT TO DO IF YOU FEEL NUMB OR DOWN

Sometimes life feels heavy, like you're moving through fog. Getting out of bed, answering texts, or even brushing your teeth feels like climbing a mountain. The things you used to love — soccer, painting, hanging out, music — don't spark joy anymore.

It's not always sadness. Sometimes it's emptiness. You go through the motions but feel detached, like everything's happening in grayscale.

That's not laziness or "just being moody." For many girls, these are signs of depression — even if nobody says the word out loud.

***

What Depression Can Look Like (and What It's Not)

Depression doesn't always show up as crying all the time or hiding under a blanket. Sometimes it's irritability, zoning out, or feeling constantly drained.

You might:
- snap at people over tiny things
- pull away from friends or stop replying to texts
- sleep too much or barely at all
- lose interest in food — or eat more for comfort
- struggle to focus, letting schoolwork pile up.

And then comes the guilt — for falling behind, for disappointing people, for not being able to "just shake it off."

When everyone else seems fine, it's easy to believe you're broken or weak. But depression isn't a choice, and you can't just "snap out of it." You can have good things in your life — friends, hobbies, achievements — and still feel empty inside.

Needing help doesn't make you fragile. Asking for it is one of the bravest things you can do.

***

How It Feels Inside

Depression can distort your thoughts. It whispers:

"You're not good enough."

"You're a burden."

"No one would understand."

Those thoughts *feel* true, but they're symptoms — not facts. Depression changes how your brain processes hope, motivation, and pleasure. It's like trying to see clearly through foggy glass: the world hasn't changed, but your ability to see it has.

You're not imagining it. You're fighting a real, internal storm.

***

Recognizing the Signs Early

Here's what to watch for in yourself or someone you care about:

- a persistent feeling of sadness or emptiness that lasts for weeks

- loss of interest in favorite activities

- constant tiredness or low energy

- difficulty concentrating or making decisions

- changes in eating or sleeping habits

- feelings of worthlessness or guilt

- thoughts that life doesn't matter or that you'd rather disappear.

Even if you relate to only a few of these, it's worth paying attention. You don't have to hit "rock bottom" before asking for help.

***

Why Shame Keeps You Silent

Depression loves isolation. It makes you feel like you're the only one feeling this way, or that everyone else is coping better. You might tell yourself, *It's just a phase,* or *I shouldn't feel this way; I have it good.*

But you can be grateful and still be struggling. You can smile in photos and still be hurting. You can be strong and still need help.

That's not a contradiction — that's being human.

Small Steps That Actually Help

You don't need to fix everything at once. Start small — the smallest steps count.

Reach out to someone you trust: a parent, counselor, coach, or teacher. You don't have to give a whole speech. Try something simple like:

"I don't feel like myself lately."

"I've been exhausted and down."

"I think I need help."

If saying it feels impossible, send a message or leave a note. The words don't have to be perfect — they need to be honest.

Adults often want to help but don't always know how to start. Give them a chance to listen.

If you ever have thoughts of hurting yourself, or you feel you might act on them, get help right away. Tell an adult, call your local emergency number, or contact a crisis line. You deserve immediate support.

***

Tracking What You Feel

Depression can make time blur together. Keeping a *mood journal* can help you see patterns and notice minor improvements you might otherwise miss.

Each day, jot down a few words, colors, or symbols to describe your mood. You can also rate your energy on a scale of 1–10 or draw faces that reflect how you feel.

Over time, you might notice triggers — stressful weeks, social pressure, lack of sleep — or find what helps: music, movement, rest, or being outdoors.

When things feel unpredictable, tracking shows you that your feelings *do* change — even a little — and that's hope in motion.

***

Creating Tiny Anchors

Small routines can make a huge difference. They don't "cure" depression, but they give your mind structure and a sense of control.

One girl started walking her dog at the same time every day. That 20-minute routine became her anchor. Another made playlists for different moods — one for anger, one for when she felt hopeless, and one for focus.

These simple rituals gave shape to her day, reminding her she could still do *something*, even when motivation was gone.

> **Here are a few other gentle anchors you can try:**
>
> - open your curtains first thing in the morning to let in light
>
> - drink water and eat something small before noon
>
> - stretch for two minutes
>
> - text one safe friend a simple "hey."

Small doesn't mean meaningless. These moments build tiny cracks of light into dark days.

Real Stories, Real Hope

One girl described months of feeling "empty" and disconnected. She thought needing help meant she was broken. One day, she finally told her aunt, *"I feel weird and tired all the time."* Her aunt helped her find a therapist. At first, she barely spoke in sessions—but slowly, just having someone listen began to lift the weight.

Another student shared that therapy wasn't a magical fix but gave her language for what she was feeling. Naming the pain made it less scary.

Recovery doesn't always look like joy bursting through the clouds. It's often quiet—finishing homework again, laughing once in a while, noticing that you feel *a little less heavy* than last week.

***

What Recovery Really Looks Like

Getting better from depression doesn't mean waking up one day, suddenly happy. It means noticing progress in small, tangible ways:

- laughing at a silly TikTok

- finishing a meal

- getting dressed even when you don't want to

- showing up to school, even if you feel off.

For some, progress means therapy or learning coping skills. For others, it's surrounding themselves with people who genuinely care—both count.

Healing isn't linear. Some days will feel like steps backward. That doesn't erase your progress—it just means you're human.

***

IF YOU EVER FEEL UNSAFE

If you ever think about hurting yourself or wonder whether things will ever get better, *please reach out immediately.* You don't need to face those thoughts alone, and you don't need to wait until they feel "serious enough."

> **Here are options available anytime:**
>
> **988 Suicide & Crisis Lifeline (U.S.)** — call or text **988** for free support, any time.
> **Crisis Text Line** — text **HELLO** to **741741** to connect with a trained listener.
> **Teen Line** — call **800-852-8336** or text **TEEN** to **839863** to talk with another teen.
> **findahelpline.com** — for local numbers worldwide.

You deserve help and a chance to feel okay again. There's always someone on the other end who cares.

***

Finding Your Safe People

Choosing who to talk to can feel confusing. You might worry about being a burden or about not being taken seriously. But you don't need to pick the "perfect" person. You need someone who listens.

Think about:

- Who stays calm when others panic?

- Who has checked in on you before?

- Who respects your privacy and doesn't gossip?

- Who makes you feel lighter after talking to them?

That person could be a counselor, teacher, coach, parent, aunt, older sibling, or even someone like your school librarian or art teacher. You don't have to be close friends—you need trust.

If talking in person feels too hard, start with a message:

"Hey, I've been feeling really off and could use someone to talk to."

"Things have been rough lately. Can we meet after school?"

"I don't know where to start, but I need help."

It doesn't have to be long. Just reaching out is enough to start a change.

***

If They Don't Get It (At First)

Not every adult knows how to respond ideally. Some may try to fix things too fast or brush it off because they don't understand what depression feels like.

If your first attempt doesn't go well, that doesn't mean you failed. It means you need a *different listener*.

You can try again by saying:

"I didn't feel understood last time — can we try again?"

"That conversation didn't come out right. I want to explain better."

You might have to reach out more than once, but the right person *will* listen.

One student felt too scared to talk in person, so she emailed her science teacher. That simple message led to after-school check-ins and, eventually, professional support. Another teen texted a mental health chatline and found comfort within minutes.

Sometimes even telling a friend, *"I'm not okay lately,"* opens a door. That small truth can connect you to help faster than you think.

***

Keep Going — You're Not Alone

Depression tells you that nobody cares. That you'll always feel this way. That asking for help is too embarrassing or pointless.

But that's depression lying to you.

You don't have to wait until your pain feels "valid enough." If something inside you feels off, you're allowed to ask for care. You deserve to feel better.

Even on days when your hope feels paper-thin, keep reaching out. Keep talking. Keep taking small steps.

Your story matters — every single word of it. And no matter what your mind tells you, you're never alone in this.

***

BUILDING YOUR PERSONAL COPING SKILLS PLAYLIST

When everything feels like too much, a "coping skills playlist" can be your reset button — a collection of tools you can reach for when thoughts spiral, moods dip, or life feels heavy.

Think of it as a personalized survival kit for your emotions — a mix of activities, small rituals, and grounding habits that help you feel steady again.

Coping isn't about ignoring feelings or pretending everything's fine. It's about giving yourself options — real, practical ways to soothe your body, calm your mind, and reconnect to what matters.

Everyone's playlist will look different. Some people need movement; others need quiet. The best playlists include a little of both — something for your **body, mind, connections,** and **creativity.**

***

Body: Calming the Physical Storm

Your body is often the first place anxiety or sadness shows up — tight shoulders, shallow breathing, jittery hands. Simple physical actions can signal to your brain that you're safe.

> **Try:**
>
> - stretching your arms and rolling your shoulders
>
> - walking around the block or your room
>
> - lying down and focusing on deep, slow breaths
>
> - stepping outside for a change of air
>
> - noticing your feet on the ground or splashing cool water on your face.

These small moves might seem basic, but they reset your nervous system and help your body tell your brain, *"We're okay."*

***

Mind: Regrounding Your Thoughts

When your thoughts feel tangled or loud, grounding techniques can bring you back to the present.

Try the "5-4-3-2-1" method:

- Name **5 things** you see.

- **4 things** you can touch.

- **3 things** you hear.

- **2 things** you smell.

- **1 thing** you can taste.

It sounds simple, but it's powerful — it pulls you out of your head and into the moment.

You can also:

- Listen to a short guided meditation (there are tons of free ones online).

- Repeat short affirmations like, *"I'm doing my best,"* or *"This feeling will pass."*

- Write down three small good things from your day — even something like *"the sun felt warm,"* or *"my friend made me laugh."*

When your mind starts spiraling, small, grounding thoughts can help you find a foothold.

***

Connection: Reaching Out for Relief

Sometimes the best coping tool is another person. Connection doesn't always have to mean a deep talk — even light, silly moments count.

Try:

- sending a funny meme or "thinking of you" text

- petting your dog or cat for a few minutes

- saying hi to someone in the hallway

- thanking someone who helped you.

Tiny acts of connection remind your brain that you're not alone — that life still has warmth and meaning, even in challenging moments.

If you're struggling to reach out, start small: a heart emoji, a shared song, or a short *"Hey, how are you?"* is enough.

***

Creativity: Expressing, Not Suppressing

When words aren't enough, creative outlets can help feelings move through you instead of getting stuck.

Try:
- doodling, painting, or crafting — no pressure to make it pretty
- baking something simple
- curating a playlist that fits your mood
- taking photos of small things that make you smile
- writing poetry, journaling, or making a voice note to yourself.

Creativity gives you space to express emotions without judgment. You don't have to post or share it — this is just for *you*.

***

How to Build (and Keep) Your Playlist

Your coping playlist is all about experimentation. Start by writing down 10–15 things that sound doable — not what you *think* should work, but what you're actually willing to try.

Then, test one strategy a day and note how it feels. If something doesn't help, cross it off and replace it. Maybe yoga isn't your thing, but dancing alone in your room allows. Maybe journaling feels forced, but music always works.

Keep your list flexible — what helps now might change later. Growth means adapting, not sticking to one formula.

Reflection Prompt:
After trying a coping skill, write down:
"How did I feel before? What changed after?"

You might notice that even five minutes of breathing or a walk shifts something inside you. Over time, you'll discover which tools are your go-tos and which ones you can retire.

***

Real-Life Playlists

Here are a few ways other girls have made their coping playlists:

The Five-Minute Morning Routine: splash water on your face, play a favorite song, stretch, and set one small goal — like *"just show up."*

The School-Day Plan: a doodle notebook for lunch, calming videos saved for after class, and affirmations taped inside a binder.

The Free & Simple Version: watching clouds, counting backward from 100 by sevens, or texting a cousin a random question.

Playlists can be short or long. Some days you'll only manage one thing — that's still success.

***

Keep It Handy

Store your playlist where you can reach it fast:

- A Notes app on your phone.

- A small notebook in your bag.

- Sticky notes on your mirror.

Add new ideas as you go. Let it evolve with you.

***

The Bigger Picture

Coping isn't about "fixing" everything instantly. It's about lightening the load enough to keep going.

Each time you use a healthy coping skill, you're teaching yourself something powerful: *I can help myself through hard things.*

That's real resilience — not never struggling, but knowing you can handle the storm when it comes.

Mental health takes practice and patience, not perfection. Showing up for yourself — even in the smallest ways — is already enough.

> **Try This:**
>
> In your journal, title a page *"My Coping Skills Playlist."*
> Draw four boxes labeled:
> **Body | Mind | Connection | Creativity.**

Fill each one with at least three ideas. Keep adding whenever you discover something new that helps.

Before Reflection:

Take a deep breath—you've faced hard truths in this chapter. Now, give yourself credit for showing up with honesty and courage.

Reflection: Your Inner Strength

Every time you face what's hard instead of hiding from it, you prove your strength. Healing isn't about pretending everything's fine—it's about taking small, honest steps toward peace. You're already doing better than you think.

Keep showing up for yourself—the strongest version of you is already in motion.

Chapter 2

Owning Your Identity

Finding Your Place When You Feel "Different"

Picture this: you walk into a noisy classroom and scan for a seat. Your backpack suddenly feels heavier. Maybe your accent stands out when you say "hi," or your sketchbook is full of anime drawings instead of football doodles. Your outfit may not match what's trending on TikTok. You feel hopeful and anxious all at once — trying to blend in while wondering if you ever really will.

One reader once told me, *"Sometimes I feel like I'm on the outside of every group."* That feeling — of standing just beyond the circle — is a shared experience for many people, including you.

***

AM I "TOO DIFFERENT"? — NAVIGATING QUESTIONS OF BELONGING

Feeling "not like everyone else" can be lonely. And often, the harshest voice isn't the one around you — it's the one inside your own head. The whisper that says, *"You're too weird," "You'll never fit in,"* or *"No one gets you."*

That loneliness grows louder when nobody seems to share your quirks or background — whether that's speaking another language, loving coding or calligraphy, having ADHD, a chronic illness, or simply not matching the usual social mold. It could also be about your sexual orientation, gender identity, or any other aspect of your unique self.

Some differences are visible — your skin, your hair, your faith, how you dress. Others live beneath the surface — anxiety, cultural identity, creative passions that no one else seems to share. Each of them can make you wonder if there's a place where you truly belong.

***

You're Not Alone in Feeling Different

I've heard a lot of stories.

One reader who adored manga described eating lunch alone while everyone else talked about sports. She said she felt like she'd been dropped into the wrong world. Another girl, the only one in her class who wore a hijab, described the sting of stares and the weight of silence — not bullying exactly, but invisibility. Both asked me the same question in different ways: *"Is being different always going to make me feel left out?"*

Here's what I told them — and what I want you to hear too: **feeling out of place doesn't mean there's something wrong with you.** In fact, it often means you have something unique and valuable to offer.

***

The Truth About Fitting In

During adolescence, almost everyone wants to belong. It's one of the strongest human needs — to be seen, included, accepted. So when you stand out, even for good reasons, it can feel like you're being left behind. That urge to blend in can make you hide the very things that make you shine.

But here's the paradox: the same things that make you "different" are often the very things that make you *magnetic.*

Your accent, your curiosity, your creativity, your sense of humor — these aren't barriers; they're your signature. The world doesn't need more copies; it requires your original story.

It might not feel like a superpower yet — right now, it might just feel awkward or lonely — but every person who ever made an impact started by standing out.

***

How to Start Seeing Your Uniqueness as Strength.

Try this mindset shift: instead of asking *"Why don't I fit in?"* ask *"How can my uniqueness make a difference?"* Your differences are not weaknesses; they are your superpowers waiting to be unleashed.

If you're the only coder in your class, you could start a robotics club.

If you're obsessed with vintage fashion, you could inspire friends to explore thrift stores.

If your faith, accent, or background feels misunderstood, you're the bridge that helps others learn.

When you stop shrinking your differences and start exploring what they can offer, belonging becomes something you *build,* not something you wait for.

***

Interactive Exercise: Reframe Your Differences

Grab a sheet of paper and fold it in half.

On the left, list three things that make you "different." They can be anything — your culture, interests, temperament, beliefs, sense of humor, or how you see the world.

On the right, rewrite each one as a **strength.**

Example:

- *"I speak another language"* - *"I can connect with people across cultures and understand different perspectives."*

- *"I love anime"* - *"My imagination and creativity help me tell stories others relate to."*

- *"I'm quiet"* - *"I notice details others miss and make people feel heard."*

Then, reflect for a minute: when has being different actually helped you or someone else?

Maybe you reached out to a new student because you remembered what it felt like to be the outsider. Your unique idea turned a dull group project into something original. Or perhaps you comforted a friend because your own struggles helped you understand what they were going through.

Write down one moment when your difference had a positive impact —
even a small one.

***

The Myth of the "Normal" Teen

Spoiler: there's no such thing.

The "normal" everyone chases is a moving target — shaped by social media,
peer pressure, and whatever's trending this week. Everyone's pretending a
little. Even the people who look confident are often wondering, *"Am I doing
this right?"*

The truth is, belonging doesn't mean sameness. It means being accepted *as
you are.*

Trying to erase your quirks just to fit in might work for a while, but it
costs too much — your energy, your authenticity, your joy. Real belonging
happens when you can be yourself without fear of rejection.

***

Creating Belonging (Instead of Waiting for It)

If you can't find a space that feels like home, you can create one. Start a
club, initiate a conversation, or suggest an activity that aligns with your
interests. Don't be afraid to take the first step in creating a community that
celebrates your uniqueness.

If there's no manga club, ask a teacher how to start one.

If you love debate but nobody in your friend group does, sign up anyway — your next friend might be waiting there.

If you notice someone sitting alone, invite them to join you. Sometimes the simple words *"Want to sit with me?"* are the beginning of a whole new story.

Building belonging doesn't mean forcing connections with everyone. It means finding your people — the ones who see you, not just your surface.

You don't have to share every interest to connect. Curiosity, kindness, and openness build bridges faster than popularity or matching outfits ever could.

***

Real Stories, Real Courage

One teen told me she finally stopped hiding her sketchbook and started drawing in class — quietly, at first. A few weeks later, another student asked to see her work. Soon, they were designing characters together. That tiny moment of bravery opened a door she didn't know existed.

Another girl decided to wear her cultural jewelry even though no one else did. She was nervous at first, but ended up getting real, kind questions—and discovered people were curious, not critical.

Owning who you are doesn't mean you'll never feel out of place again, but it changes the story you tell yourself about it. Instead of thinking, *"I don't belong,"* you begin to realize, *"I'm still finding where I fit — and that's okay."*

> **Reflection Prompt:**
> In your journal, write about a time you felt different or out of place. What made you think that way? What did you learn about yourself through it? Then, finish this sentence:
> *"Something that makes me unique — and I'm starting to appreciate — is..."*

Even if it feels small, claim it. Saying it out loud helps it take root.

***

One Last Thought

Feeling "too different" doesn't mean you're broken or behind. It means you're human — still unfolding, still learning where you fit in the world.

Owning your story isn't about being loud or proving yourself. It's about standing in quiet confidence, knowing your differences are not flaws to fix but gifts to grow into.

Your "different" might be precisely what makes someone else feel seen for the first time.

So, don't dim your colors to match the crowd. The world needs your full spectrum.

***

CULTURE, FAITH, AND FAMILY — HONORING YOUR UNIQUE STORY

Your culture, faith, and family shape how you see the world. Sometimes those roots feel like a warm, steady foundation — comforting, familiar, grounding. Other times, they can feel heavy, especially when expectations collide with your personal dreams.

Your parents imagine a practical career while your heart leans toward art, music, or writing. You may miss hangouts or school events because of religious observances or family responsibilities. Balancing what matters at home with what excites you personally can feel like a tug-of-war — one that pulls at both your loyalty and your independence.

***

Living Between Two Worlds

For many teens, living between cultures is the norm. You might speak one language at home and another at school. You might switch the way you talk, dress, or express yourself depending on who's around.

At home, you help make traditional meals or celebrate holidays that classmates have never heard of. At school, you might deal with mispronounced names, curious questions, or jokes about your lunch.

Often, it's not the curiosity that stings — it's the sense that nobody truly *gets* what it's like to live in both worlds at once.

***

The Weight of Expectations

That in-between space can feel exhausting. You may feel out of sync with your family if you like different clothes or music. You may feel out of sync with your peers if you keep traditions they don't understand.

Trying to explain your culture or faith to others can be awkward, especially when people make insensitive comments or treat your background like a curiosity. Those moments can make you want to hide parts of yourself — to shrink what's precious so it doesn't get questioned.

But you don't have to hide.

***

Speaking Up with Confidence

Sometimes, a few calm, prepared responses make those moments easier.

> If someone comments on your lunch, you might say,
> *"This is special to my family — want to hear more?"*
> If a question crosses a line, you can say,
> *"That's not cool. This means something to me."*

You decide how much you want to share. Some people are genuinely curious; others might need a reminder to be respectful.

And remember — you don't owe anyone your story. Setting boundaries isn't rude; it's healthy.

> If a question feels too personal, you can say,
> *"I'd rather not talk about that right now."*
> and change the subject.

Not every comment deserves your time or explanation. Protecting your peace matters more than educating everyone else.

***

Pride and Connection

Even with the challenges, many girls discover deep pride in their heritage and faith. These roots hold memories, values, and lessons that can guide you through life.

One student introduced **Lunar New Year** to her class, sharing red envelopes and stories from her family — what started as a small presentation turned into a celebration that her whole school looked forward to.

Another girl, who felt torn between her parents' culture and her American friends, started a club for students "living in between." They swapped stories, foods, and traditions — and for the first time, she didn't have to explain herself.

Online spaces can help too. Safe communities — like moderated Discord servers, forums, or youth groups for multicultural teens — can offer a place to connect without constantly justifying who you are.

Your identity is richer because of the worlds you bridge. Sharing your traditions, stories, and beliefs gives others a window into your strength and resilience.

***

Balancing Family and Freedom

Family expectations don't always disappear — especially in cultures that value collective goals, responsibility, or respect for elders. You might feel torn between honoring your family and making choices that feel true to you.

Some moments will require compromise — like adjusting how you explain your dreams or agreeing to small traditions that matter to them. Other times, you'll have to gently stand your ground — saying, *"I hear you, but this is what's right for me."*

One girl dreamed of studying design, but her parents pushed her toward medicine. She found balance by taking a science track in school while volunteering at a community art studio. Over time, her parents saw her passion and began to understand that creativity was her calling, not rebellion.

Every family's journey looks different, but the same truth holds: you can respect where you come from without losing yourself in it.

Owning your culture and faith doesn't mean choosing one over the other — it means learning to carry both with pride.

***

QUESTIONING YOUR IDENTITY — WHO CAN YOU TRUST WITH YOUR TRUTH?

However it looks, figuring things out doesn't mean something's wrong with you.

It means you're growing. Discovering who you are is rarely a straight path.

Some days you feel entirely sure of yourself; other days you question everything — who you're attracted to, which pronouns feel right, or whether the beliefs you grew up with still fit.

You may be noticing a new kind of crush.

The faith or routines that once felt comforting now feel confusing.

Maybe you're just realizing there's more to your story than you've ever said out loud.

Whatever it looks like, **you're allowed to take your time.** There's no deadline for understanding yourself, and no rule that says you owe anyone an announcement before you're ready.

Curiosity, fear, excitement, and uncertainty can all coexist. It's okay to feel every one of them.

***

Before You Share — Check In With Yourself

Wanting to tell someone can feel freeing *and* terrifying. Before you share something personal — whether it's about your beliefs, gender, sexuality, or identity — pause and ask yourself a few grounding questions:

- Am I looking for comfort, advice, or to be heard?

- Do I trust this person to handle my words with care and privacy?

- Is this the right time and place, or should I wait?

- Am I ready for any kind of reaction — positive, neutral, or difficult?

Choosing when to share isn't about secrecy; it's about safety.

Your truth belongs to you, and you get to decide who holds it.

***

Finding the Right Words

If talking feels impossible, start by writing.

Type out your thoughts in a private note, record a voice memo, or journal freely. Seeing your feelings written down can bring clarity — and if you decide to talk later, you'll already know what matters most to say.

> **When you're ready, you can begin small:**
> *"I want to tell you something, but I'm nervous."*
> *"I'm figuring out who I am, and I'd really appreciate your support."*
> *"There's something personal I've been thinking about — can we talk?"*

For family, you might say,

> *"Can we talk privately? This is hard for me to say, but it's important."*
> If it's at school or with an adult, a short, respectful boundary helps:
> *"This is personal, and I'd appreciate your understanding."*

You don't need to spill everything at once. Sometimes even saying, "I've been thinking about who I am lately" is enough to open the door.

***

Not Everyone Will React the Same Way

Some people will meet your honesty with love.

Others may respond with confusion, silence, or denial — not because you did anything wrong, but because they don't yet know how to handle what they've heard.

That's painful, and it's okay to grieve those reactions.

Take a breath. Remind yourself: *their response doesn't define me.*

If someone outs you, rejects you, or uses your vulnerability against you, it's not your fault. Their reaction reflects their limits, not your value.

This is when leaning on other supports becomes crucial. A school counselor, a supportive teacher, a youth group leader, or a friend who listens can help you process and plan next steps.

***

If Things Go Wrong

Suppose a conversation goes badly or you feel unsafe. In that case, there are safe, confidential resources that can help — no matter where you live. *(See Chapter 1 for a full list of trusted hotlines and support lines.)*

You are never alone, and help is always available. Even a single supportive message or call can remind you that you're not alone, even if people nearby don't understand yet.

***

Acceptance Often Comes from Unexpected Places

Sometimes, the most understanding people aren't the ones you expect.

It might be a teacher who quietly asks if you're okay, a cousin who checks in, or a friend online who tells you they've felt the same way.

If the first person you tell doesn't get it, keep going. You deserve to find listeners who see your courage and celebrate your honesty.

One girl shared that her first coming-out conversation ended in silence — but a week later, her art teacher left a sticky note on her desk that said, *"Thanks for trusting me. You're brave."* That single note became her reminder that support exists, even if it takes time to find.

Reflection Prompt:

- Write down a few names — people who make you feel safe, heard, or respected.

- What qualities do they share? Calmness? Humor? Kindness? Reliability?

Then, finish this sentence in your journal:
"I feel most like myself when I'm with people who..."

Your answer will guide you toward the communities that truly deserve you.

***

Your Story, Your Timing

Whether you're questioning, defining, or simply exploring, your story is still unfolding — and that's okay. You can be proud of yourself even while things are uncertain.

You don't have to rush clarity. You don't have to explain everything. And you definitely don't have to face it alone.

Keep reaching for the people and spaces that make you feel seen, not small.

You are not "too much," "too different," or "too complicated." You are real, and you are worthy — precisely as you are, in this moment.

***

FINDING YOUR PEOPLE — BUILDING REAL CONNECTION ONLINE AND OFF

Discovering a community that resonates with you can be a transformative experience. In this place, your voice is not just tolerated but truly wanted. This difference is significant. One space can leave you feeling drained and insignificant. At the same time, another can fill you with a sense of energy and belonging that lingers long after you've left.

Perhaps you've been in groups where you felt compelled to be quieter, where every conversation felt like walking on eggshells, or where you had to censor yourself to fit in. This can be exhausting and is not the kind of connection you deserve. True belonging occurs when you don't have to shrink or conceal what matters most to you. It's about showing up as you are, quirks and all, and knowing that some people genuinely want to see the real you.

Remember, it's OK to start small. The important thing is to start somewhere.

Begin by looking for groups that align with your interests or parts of your identity. Love books, robotics, art, activism, or debate? See what's happening at school: clubs like Gender & Sexuality Alliances (GSAs), cultural groups, or a Black Student Union can be lifelines.

If nothing like that exists yet, talk to a teacher or counselor about starting one. Community doesn't have to begin big—it can start with three people and a group chat in the hallway. Don't underestimate a simple invitation:

"Hey, I noticed you like this, too. Want to start something together?"

Even virtual circles count. You could run a small book club on Zoom, start a Discord server for fandom art, or plan a movie night that brings together friends from different schools. What matters isn't the format—it's the shared sense of being seen.

***

Online Doesn't Mean Unreal

Online spaces open up even more possibilities, especially if your town or school feels small. Look for teen-friendly, **moderated communities**—Discord servers with clear rules, book or art groups, or school-sponsored forums that require sign-in.

If you join an online group, always keep privacy in mind. Never share your home address, phone number, school name, or private photos, no matter how friendly someone seems. And remember—if a conversation makes you uncomfortable or someone pressures you to reveal things, you don't owe them a single answer.

Block, report, and move on. Most platforms give you those tools for a reason.

Check the Vibe

Community isn't just about who's there—it's about how you feel there.

Ask yourself:

- Do I leave this space feeling understood and energized?

- Or do I feel tense, invisible, or drained?

If it's the second, that's your cue to step back. Belonging should never feel like a performance.

Sometimes you'll find your people where you least expect—an after-school art club, a quiet online book group, or a small gathering at your faith center. Genuine connection doesn't demand you to be loud or perfect; it just asks you to be present and real.

> **Try a quick reflection after hangouts or chats:**
> *"How did I feel afterward?"*
> Notice patterns. Choose the spaces that leave you feeling fuller—not smaller.

***

Create the Space You Need

Starting your own group might sound intimidating, but it often begins with something simple.

One reader formed a small group chat for girls of color after noticing how isolated they felt in classes dominated by cliques. It started with trading memes and venting about school—but quickly became a space for support, advice, and laughter.

Another student launched a graphic-novel fandom club. She printed a few flyers, handed them out in homeroom, and within weeks, her club had regular meetings and an online art challenge.

If "starting a club" feels like too much, start micro: host a virtual study group, a creative collab, or a "music swap" thread with long-distance friends. Communities grow naturally when people feel safe enough to show up as themselves.

***

When Online Becomes a Lifeline

Chosen families aren't limited by geography. Many teens find them through activism accounts, supportive creators, or online communities built for inclusion.

Look for spaces that feel balanced—where moderators enforce boundaries, kindness is a rule, and nobody pressures you to share more than you want. A promising sign is when a group posts **rules, has active moderators, and includes clear privacy reminders.**

If you're unsure where to start, ask a teacher, counselor, or friend for suggestions. The right community can feel like a soft landing—a place where you're reminded that you belong.

***

Fitting In Is Overrated—Being Celebrated Is the Goal

As you connect with people who get the real you, you'll start to see that "fitting in" is never the prize. Feeling safe enough to be *yourself*—that's the real win.

If the group you need doesn't exist yet, don't be afraid to build it. There's someone else out there waiting for precisely the kind of space you wish existed.

One day, someone will thank you for being brave enough to start it.

Before you move on, remember this: finding your people means finding spaces that accept *all* of you—not just the parts others find easy to understand.

Whether it's in a classroom, a group chat, or a cozy Discord channel, real belonging grows where honesty, laughter, and respect all live together. Keep building circles that make you feel bigger inside, not smaller.

Before Reflection:

Pause here and think about what truly makes you *you*. No filters, no comparisons—just your authentic, growing self.

Reflection: Becoming Who You Already Are

You don't have to chase who you're supposed to be—you're already becoming her. Every time you tell the truth about what matters to you, you build a stronger, more grounded version of yourself. That's what absolute confidence looks like.

The world doesn't need another copy—it needs your original spark.

Chapter 3

Communication Glow-Up

Finding Your Voice and Setting Boundaries

Building authentic connections is powerful—but keeping them healthy takes skill.

Once you find your people, the next step is learning how to express what you need, speak up with confidence, and set boundaries that protect your energy.

Because genuine connection isn't just about being included—it's about being *heard*.

***

SAYING WHAT YOU MEAN—SCRIPTS FOR TRICKY CONVERSATIONS

Ever lie awake replaying a talk that didn't go the way you wanted? Maybe you let something slide that bothered you, or froze when someone crossed a line. Just thinking about bringing it up makes your chest tighten and your palms sweat. *What if they get mad? What if I sound dramatic? What if my voice shakes?*

Feeling nervous before a challenging conversation is totally normal. Speaking up for yourself takes courage—especially when you care about how the other person might react. But honest communication is the only way relationships really work. Without it, misunderstandings pile up and resentment quietly builds. You deserve to be heard—not so that other people won't get upset, but because your feelings matter.

***

Clarity Isn't Conflict

Being direct doesn't mean being harsh. It means being transparent and open about what you think, feel, and hope will change. When you say what you mean—calmly and specifically—people get to know the real you, and trust grows from that honesty. It takes vulnerability, yes, but courage isn't about not feeling scared; it's about showing up anyway.

Every time you speak clearly, you strengthen your voice and your self-respect.

When a talk feels intimidating, start simple. You can say, *"I really need to talk to you about something that's been on my mind."* That one sentence signals this conversation matters.

Then focus on describing how something affects you rather than accusing. The *"I feel ___ when ___ because ___ "* structure helps keep it grounded.

For example, if a friend keeps canceling plans, you might want to say, *"It's fine, don't worry,"* even when it's not. A clearer, kinder version would be:

"Hey, I've noticed our plans keep getting canceled, and it makes me feel unimportant. I really value our time—can we try to make plans that stick?"

See the difference? The first hides your feelings; the second invites an honest fix.

Or if you're struggling with a teacher's assignment, try, *"I've been having trouble with this and could use some extra help. Is there a time we could meet?"* That's not bothering anyone—it's taking ownership of your learning.

Even with parents, it helps to trade eye rolls or slammed doors for words that show understanding. You could say, *"I get why you have this rule, but I see it differently. Can we talk about how I'm feeling?"* They might still say no, but they'll hear your maturity—and that matters.

***

Keeping Calm When Things Get Tense

During a tough conversation, breathe slowly and remind yourself that you don't need to rush. Keep your tone steady and your posture relaxed. Use "I" statements instead of "you always..." or "you never..."—that slight shift helps the other person listen rather than get defensive.

If things start to heat up, it's OK to say, *"Can we take a break and come back to this when we're calmer?"*

You're not quitting—you're protecting the conversation. And if your voice shakes or your eyes water, that's not a failure. It's honesty, and people often respond better to that than to polished perfection.

***

Prepare, Don't Over-Plan

Before a hard talk, take a few minutes to jot your thoughts in a notebook or your Notes app.

- What do you really want to say?

- What's your main goal—to clear the air, ask for change, or be understood?

Imagine how the other person might feel or respond, and plan how you'll stay calm if they interrupt or disagree. Writing a quick opening line—something like, *"I really want to explain what's been bothering me,"*—helps you start strong.

You can even practice out loud. Try saying it in front of a mirror or while walking. Hearing your words makes them feel more natural, and soon your confidence will start catching up to your courage.

***

If It Doesn't Go Perfectly

Sometimes you'll do everything "right" and it still won't land the way you hoped. The other person might react defensively, change the subject, or not understand. That doesn't erase the bravery it took to speak up.

You can always pause and say, *"I'm not trying to argue—I just want to share how I feel,"* or come back later when emotions settle.

Afterward, take a few quiet minutes to reflect: What went well? What was harder than expected? Did I say what mattered most? Every tough conversation teaches you something about how you communicate—and how you want to be heard.

Speaking up doesn't make you rude or dramatic—it makes you *real*. Each time you express yourself honestly, even if your voice trembles, you're proving that your feelings deserve a place in the conversation. That's how absolute confidence begins—one honest talk at a time.

Up next, we'll look at boundaries—how to set them, communicate them, and protect your energy without guilt, so your relationships stay healthy and balanced.

***

SETTING BOUNDARIES WITH FRIENDS (AND STICKING TO THEM)

Boundaries are the invisible lines that protect your comfort, energy, and self-respect. Think of them like a personal bubble—one that shows what's OK and what's not, both physically and emotionally. They're not about shutting people out; they're about caring for yourself, even when it feels awkward.

Sometimes you notice a boundary has been crossed before you can even name it. Maybe a friend pressures you to share passwords, expects instant replies, or gets hurt when you ask for alone time. If you often feel drained after hanging out or anxious about saying "no," your body is sending you a signal that something's off.

Recognizing those moments is the first step. Pay attention to situations that leave you uneasy—being pushed to overshare, doing favors you don't want, or feeling guilty for wanting space. If someone insists on knowing every detail of your life or gets upset when you unplug, that's not closeness—it's overstepping. Even small things, like borrowing your stuff without asking or tagging you in photos you don't like, can slowly chip away at your sense of comfort.

You don't need a dramatic blow-up to draw a line; your feelings are reason enough.

Saying no can feel risky, especially if you fear disappointing people or being labeled "selfish."

But protecting your limits is a form of self-respect. The way you say it matters—be clear and kind, not defensive or apologetic. Try gentle but direct lines like:

"I'm not comfortable sharing my password, but I trust you."

"I can't text all night—I need to unplug."

"I want to be there for you, but I also need some time for myself."

They may feel stiff at first, but they get easier with use—kind of like building a muscle you didn't know you had.

Sometimes, when you start setting limits, friends might push back. They may tease you, act hurt, or guilt-trip you with lines like, *"Why are you being distant?"* Stay steady. You can reply, *"I care about you, but I need this for my well-being."* If they keep pushing, calmly repeat your limit:

"I'm not shutting you out—I just need space to recharge." You don't need to defend yourself endlessly. If a friendship only works when you ignore your needs, it might be time to pull back. Healthy connections will respect your boundaries, even if it takes a slight adjustment.

If setting limits feels especially hard—especially with people close to you—start small. Say no to a little thing: skip a late-night FaceTime when you're tired, decline a tag in a photo you dislike, or keep your hoodie to yourself if you don't want to lend it. Notice how it feels. Most true friends will understand once they see it's not rejection—it's balance.

Try reflecting on this in your journal:

"What's one boundary I want to set, and what's stopping me?"
Write freely, without judging your answers. You might realize you fear conflict, rejection, or being alone. Then, draw your "boundary bubble." Inside, list what feels safe—honest talks, shared laughter, being able to say no.

Outside, write what drains you—guilt trips, pressure, or one-sided effort. Keep it somewhere private as a reminder: you're allowed to protect your space.

Choosing yourself isn't selfish—it's healthy.

You don't owe long explanations or apologies for having limits. Over time, boundaries become less about keeping people out and more about letting the right ones in—those who respect your energy, your time, and your peace. Sticking to your limits helps you stay grounded and connected to who you are, while building stronger, kinder friendships.

***

STANDING UP FOR YOURSELF—WITHOUT BEING "MEAN" OR "EXTRA"

You might worry that speaking up will get you labeled *as bossy, too sensitive,* or the one who "kills the vibe." Many girls grow up under pressure to stay quiet, keep everyone happy, and avoid rocking the boat. Maybe you've bitten your tongue when something felt unfair because you didn't want to seem rude or dramatic. There's this unspoken rule that girls should always be flexible, soft, and agreeable—never loud, never direct, never the problem.

But you probably know that staying silent when something matters to you doesn't make things better—it makes you smaller. It feels like shrinking into yourself, like melting into the background so others can stay comfortable. That quiet ache in your chest when you wish you'd spoken up? That's your intuition asking for a voice. The good news is that standing up for yourself doesn't have to mean confrontation. It's simply saying, *"My feelings count too."*

Assertiveness sits right between two extremes—passivity (letting things slide even when you're uncomfortable) and aggressiveness (pushing others to get your way). The middle ground is confidence paired with respect—for yourself and the people around you. It's about being honest without being harsh.

A powerful tool for this is the **"I statement."** Instead of blaming, it centers your emotions and needs. For example:

"I feel left out when decisions are made without me, and I'd like to be included in the group chat."

It's simple, transparent, and fair. You're not attacking the person—you're describing your experience. This invites the other person to listen rather than defend.

Your body language helps your message land. Even if your words are perfect, crossed arms or slumped shoulders can change the meaning. Try to meet people's eyes—not a stare-down, just steady contact that says, *I mean what I'm saying.* Keep your shoulders relaxed, and breathe slowly before you start.

A calm tone and open posture make you sound confident even when your heart's racing. And if your hands shake or your face gets warm? That's completely OK.

Confidence isn't the absence of fear—it's speaking despite it.

Real-Life Stories

Let's walk through a few real-life moments. Suppose your friends plan a prank that crosses a line. You don't have to laugh along or pretend you're OK with it. Try saying, *"I'm not comfortable with that—can we do something else?"*

Short. Direct. Respectful. Or when someone slips in a backhanded compliment or microaggression, you might reply, *"That comment made me uncomfortable."* You don't need a speech; even a single sentence can reset the tone.

Interruptions are another subtle way people silence you. If someone talks over you in class or during a project, try: *"I'm not finished—can I complete my thought?"* Or if your ideas keep getting brushed aside, speak up with: *"I'd like a chance to share my perspective too."* These moments, though small, teach others that your voice matters.

Start practicing where the stakes are lower—ask a classmate to return your pen, tell a sibling not to borrow your things without asking, or gently correct someone who mispronounces your name. Those micro-moments build courage for the bigger ones—like telling a friend they crossed a boundary or explaining to an adult how you really feel. In your next group hangout or class project, challenge yourself to speak up at least once—about something that matters to you.

Afterward, take a minute to reflect. What did you feel before you spoke—tension, fear, adrenaline?

How did it feel during—did time slow, did your heart pound, did your voice shake?

And afterward—relief, pride, awkwardness?

Growth often feels awkward at first. People might need time to adjust if they're used to you being quiet, but they'll learn. And so will you.

No one gets it perfect. Sometimes your words will tumble out too fast or sound sharper than you meant. Other times, you'll freeze and think of the ideal comeback later. That's OK. Every attempt is progress. Each time you speak up, you're proving to yourself—and to others—that you deserve to be heard.

Standing up for yourself isn't being mean, dramatic, or "extra." It's learning to hold your ground without losing your kindness. It's saying, *I matter too,* and trusting that the people who genuinely care about you will want to hear your truth.

Every word you speak from that place of honesty builds a quieter, stronger kind of confidence—the kind that stays with you long after the conversation ends.

***

APOLOGIZING & REPAIRING FRIENDSHIP RIFTS (EVEN IF IT'S AWKWARD)

Everyone messes up in friendships—that's part of being human. Maybe you snapped during a stressful day, shared something that wasn't yours to share, or let a friend down after promising to show up. Those moments feel heavy and uncomfortable, and it's tempting to pretend they didn't happen. But avoiding the problem rarely helps. True strength is in owning your part, and it takes courage to do so.

A genuine apology isn't about guilt or humiliation; it's about maturity. It says, *"This relationship matters to me, and I care enough to make things right."* When you take responsibility, you stop pretending everything's fine and give the friendship space to breathe again. Yes, it might be awkward at first—but that awkwardness is a bridge back to honesty.

A genuine apology goes beyond a quick "sorry." It doesn't just patch things up or rush past the hurt. It names what happened, acknowledges how it affected the other person, and shows that you plan to do better. For example:

"I'm sorry for what I said at lunch. I know it embarrassed you, and that wasn't fair. Next time, I'll think before joking like that."

That kind of honesty lands because it focuses on *their* feelings instead of your excuses. What doesn't work are half-apologies like *"I'm sorry you feel that way,"*—which shifts the blame—or *"I didn't mean it"* and *"I was just tired."*

Those comments soften your responsibility and make the hurt person feel unseen.

Some situations cut deeper—like breaking a friend's trust by sharing a secret. That requires a complete repair plan, not just an "oops." Try something like:

"I'm really sorry I told others what you shared. I broke your trust, and I understand why you're upset. I promise to keep things private moving forward—and I'll apologize to anyone I told."

It's not easy to say, but honesty rebuilds credibility faster than excuses ever could.

Sometimes the rift isn't about a single moment—it's about distance. Life gets busy, and months pass without texts or check-ins. Reconnecting takes courage, too. You might say:

"We haven't talked in ages, and I miss you. I should've reached out sooner. If you're open to it, I'd love to catch up."

The friendship might not return to exactly what it was, but that step shows sincerity. Reaching out reminds people that they mattered—and still do.

Arguments are the hardest. After a fight, both people can feel raw and defensive, waiting for the other to break the silence. Saying sorry first can feel like losing, but it's actually a sign of strength. Try:

"I regret how our argument went. I said things I shouldn't have, and I know my words hurt you. I want to make things right if you're open to it."

That apology doesn't demand instant forgiveness—it simply opens the door.

Sometimes, despite your best effort, forgiveness won't come right away—or at all. That stings, but it doesn't erase the value of your honesty. When someone isn't ready to reconnect, give them time:

"I understand if you're not ready to talk yet. I'm here whenever you are."

That line shows respect. You're not pressuring them; you're keeping the door open while showing that your apology was genuine, not just a way to ease your own guilt.

While you wait or reflect, turn inward. Ask yourself: *What did this teach me? What patterns do I notice about how I handle conflict?* Instead of replaying regret, focus on how to handle things differently next time. Every conflict reveals something—maybe you rush to defend yourself, or perhaps you tend to withdraw. Both are things you can learn from.

Remember that repairing a friendship doesn't always mean returning to how things were.

Sometimes it means finding a new rhythm, setting more precise boundaries, or realizing you've both outgrown the connection. That can be bittersweet, but it's still growth. Taking responsibility for your actions—without expecting a perfect ending—is how trust is rebuilt, either in that friendship or in future ones.

If you're unsure how to start the conversation, honesty and humility go a long way. You can say:

"This feels awkward, but I don't want to pretend nothing happened. I care about our friendship, and I want to talk."

Even if the talk feels messy, the effort matters. Most people aren't expecting perfect words; they're hoping for sincerity.

***

My Life Story – What Did I Learn?

> **Reflection Prompt:**
>
> Write about a time when a friendship got rocky. What happened? How did it feel to apologize—or to *want* to but hold back? What did the situation teach you about yourself and about how you handle conflict? What would you do differently next time?

Sometimes you'll realize that apologizing gave you closure, even if the friendship didn't survive. Sometimes you'll see how honesty strengthens the bond. Either way, reflection turns regret into growth, providing a sense of relief and comfort.

Friendships thrive on communication, not perfection. You and your friends will both make mistakes, miss cues, and say things you wish you hadn't. What matters most isn't avoiding conflict—it's being willing to face it with honesty, courage, and care. A genuine apology isn't about guilt; it's about love. And the willingness to repair, even when it's uncomfortable, is one of the most evident signs of maturity and true friendship.

Before Reflection:

Think about the conversations that shaped you this week—the ones that stretched, challenged, or empowered you.

Reflection: What You've Learned About Your Voice

Speaking up takes courage, especially when it feels uncomfortable. Every time you use your voice with honesty and respect, you make it easier for others to do the same. Keep choosing truth over silence—you were made to be heard.

Never shrink your voice to fit the room—use it to lift the room higher.

***

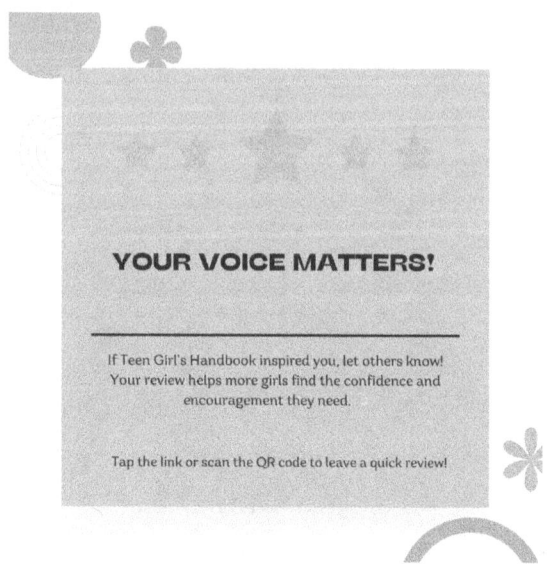

YOUR VOICE MATTERS!

If Teen Girl's Handbook inspired you, let others know!
Your review helps more girls find the confidence and
encouragement they need.

Tap the link or scan the QR code to leave a quick review!

Scan the QR code to leave your quick review!

Thank you!

Chapter 4

Self-Care That Actually Works

Beyond Bubble Baths & Face Masks

Picture this: it's midnight and you're still scrolling. Your room glows with the blue light of your screen, and the clock keeps ticking past when you *meant* to go to sleep. The next morning, you can barely drag yourself out of bed. Maybe you skip breakfast or grab something sugary, hoping it'll help you survive until lunch. By the time afternoon hits, your brain feels foggy, you're snapping at people for no reason, and even minor problems feel impossible to handle.

***

SLEEP, FOOD, AND MOOD—THE SCIENCE OF FEELING BETTER

It's easy to blame yourself for being "moody" or "lazy," but most of the time, your body is simply running on empty. Authentic self-care doesn't start with bubble baths, crystals, or expensive skincare—it begins with the basics: **sleep, food, and water.** These are the building blocks of emotional stability and focus. When they're off, *everything* else—your patience, motivation, and confidence—starts to wobble.

Skipping sleep or relying on junk food doesn't just make you tired—it can actually change how your brain works. Studies show that teens who get fewer than eight hours of sleep a night are far more vulnerable to stress, anxiety, and low mood than their well-rested peers.

Without rest, your brain struggles to regulate emotions, remember details, or think clearly. It's like trying to run your favorite app with one percent battery—eventually, it crashes.

Food plays just as significant a role. Your brain burns through more energy than any other part of your body, and it needs a steady supply of fuel to function well. Going long hours without eating, or relying on sugary snacks and caffeine, creates energy spikes followed by sharp crashes that leave you shaky or drained.

Balanced meals—especially those with protein and whole grains—help your brain make the chemicals that calm anxiety and support focus. Think of it like emotional maintenance fuel.

Foods like oatmeal, eggs, fruit, yogurt, trail mix, or nut butter are simple ways to keep your energy steady. A sandwich, smoothie, or even a handful of nuts is better than skipping entirely.

What matters isn't perfection—it's consistency.

Here's the thing: treating self-care as just "pampering" misses the point. A face mask won't fix a starving brain or replace a whole night's rest. Proper self-care is about giving your body what it actually needs to function.

You can't pour confidence or kindness from an empty tank.

How do you fix your habits when life feels too busy to change? Start small. You don't need to overhaul everything—just one or two realistic steps make a real difference.

For sleep:

- Try setting a "wind-down alarm" thirty minutes before bed—just like you'd put one to wake up.

- Turn off screens, dim the lights, or play quiet music.

- If light or noise distracts you, use a sleep mask, earplugs, or even drape a hoodie over a bright clock.

- Keep your phone across the room so you're not tempted to check it when you can't sleep.

You can also create a mini bedtime ritual—such as a short playlist, journaling, or stretching. Your brain starts to associate that pattern with rest, making it easier to unwind over time.

For food:

Focus on steady energy, not dieting or perfection. Keep quick snacks on hand for when you're too rushed to cook—whole-grain crackers, string cheese, fruit, granola bars, or trail mix. If mornings are chaos, stash instant oatmeal packets or protein bars in your backpack for a grab-and-go breakfast.

And don't underestimate **water**—dehydration quietly drains focus and energy before you even realize what's wrong.

Here's a simple trick: every time you check your phone, take a sip of water. It sounds silly, but it adds up.

If you're not sure where to start, try a quick self-check:

Sleep & Nutrition Reality Check

- Did I sleep at least 7–8 hours most nights this week?

- Did I eat something (even something small) before noon each day?

- Did I drink water when I felt tired, cranky, or unfocused?

- Did my mood dip after skipping a meal or relying only on sugar?

If you answered "not really" to most of those, you're in good company. Almost everyone struggles with this at some point—but the most minor shifts can have huge payoffs.

Take Samira, for example. She used to skip breakfast because mornings felt chaotic. She'd show up to first period cranky and unfocused, convinced she was just "bad at mornings." After a week of quick breakfasts—yogurt with fruit, a banana with peanut butter—she noticed something huge: her mood leveled out and she could actually concentrate.

One change. Big difference.

Another student swapped scrolling before bed for journaling about her day. Within two weeks, her anxiety dropped, and she fell asleep faster. You don't need a total lifestyle makeover—you need consistent, doable steps that help your body catch up with what your mind is trying to handle.

None of this has to be perfect. The point is to pay attention to what helps and to adjust slowly. Your body *remembers* what balance feels like. Once you start sleeping more and fueling yourself regularly, you'll notice your patience, focus, and creativity returning.

When you start with the basics—steady rest, consistent meals, and hydration—everything else becomes easier. Self-care isn't a luxury. It's the quiet, everyday decision to give your body and mind what they've been asking for all along.

***

SELF-CARE IN FIVE MINUTES: HACKS FOR BUSY DAYS

Self-care is often sold as expensive and time-consuming—spa days, yoga retreats, or those perfectly curated bath setups that look nothing like your real bathroom. But that's not real life for most of us. Maybe you've got practice after school, endless homework, family responsibilities, or group chats that never stop buzzing. Maybe "me time" sounds like a luxury invented by someone else. It's easy to believe there's no time left for self-care at all.

Here's the truth: you don't need hours, money, or a perfect setup to take care of yourself. Short, simple moments can work just as well—sometimes even better—than anything you see on TikTok. Just five minutes can shift your energy, calm your nerves, or help you feel like yourself again.

Think of these tiny breaks as *resets,* not escapes. You don't need to earn them. Instead of waiting for a magical free afternoon, keep a list of quick "five-minute fixes" you can pull out when you need them most.

***

Breathing That Actually Works

When stress spikes, your breath is the fastest way to hit pause. A straightforward technique is **box breathing**: inhale for four counts, hold for four, exhale for four, hold for four, and repeat. The rhythm helps slow your heartbeat and signals your nervous system that it's safe to relax.

Or try **five-finger breathing.** Hold one hand out flat. With your other index finger, trace the outline of your open hand. Inhale as you trace up each finger, exhale as you trace down. It's grounding, discreet, and can be done anywhere—at your desk, in the hallway, or even in the bathroom stall when you need a minute.

Music as a Mood Reset

Music changes your brain chemistry faster than almost anything else. Create a short playlist—one or two songs for specific moods: a power anthem for courage, something soft for calm, or a nostalgic favorite that makes you smile. Play it while brushing your teeth, walking between classes, or during a study break.

If movement helps, take it up a notch with a quick **dance break.** Close your door, turn up the volume, and move however feels good. No choreography required. Just shake it out for one song. Even three minutes of silly dancing can release tension and remind your brain what joy feels like.

***

Movement and Mini-Resets

You don't need a gym or yoga mat to move your body. Just standing up and stretching can change your mood. Try reaching your arms overhead, rolling your shoulders, or twisting gently side to side. If you're sleepy, do a few jumping jacks or walk a quick lap around your room.

Movement clears brain fog and resets your focus faster than scrolling ever will. Some teens keep a "stretch alarm" on their phones—when it buzzes, they pause, breathe, and move for sixty seconds.

Tiny habits like that can shift your energy without stealing your time.

***

Connection as Care

Self-care doesn't always mean being alone. Sometimes it means reconnecting. If you've had a hard day, text a friend a simple "thinking of you" or send a funny meme. It's a two-way lift—your message can brighten their day *and* remind you that you're not alone.

One girl told me she and her best friend made it a ritual to send each other memes after tough exams. It wasn't deep or dramatic—it just said, *"We're in this together."* Little gestures like that create emotional oxygen.

***

Build Your "Go-To" List

Grab your journal or open the Notes app and write your own five-minute care menu—things that actually help *you*. No rules. Doodle for a few minutes, squeeze a stress ball, do a skincare step that makes you feel fresh, stretch, or say a positive affirmation in the mirror.

Try each idea, then rate it: helpful, meh, or needs tweaking.

This isn't about doing everything "right"—it's about noticing what genuinely works. Some things calm your body; others lift your mood. Keep experimenting until you find the ones that feel like mini lifelines.

You can even gamify it with a **weekly challenge.** Each week, pick one new hack to try and pay attention to how it feels. Breathing helps before a big test, and music helps when mornings drag. Over time, you'll build a personalized routine that fits into the cracks of your day.

***

Real-Life Stories

One teen used box breathing in the hallway before her first big presentation. She said after two minutes, her hands stopped shaking and her voice felt steadier. Another texted a meme to a friend after failing a quiz—they laughed, talked, and suddenly the bad grade felt like just one small part of the day.

These micro-moments don't fix everything, but they remind you that you *can* shift your state of mind. They're small anchors when life feels chaotic.

***

When Five Minutes Isn't Enough

If you ever feel like the overwhelm sticks around longer than these quick fixes can handle, that's not failure—that's a sign to reach for more support. Talk to someone: a friend, family member, teacher, or counselor. Five-minute tools help you through the day, but you deserve bigger care when the hard stuff keeps coming back.

***

Start Small, Stay Consistent

Pick one hack today. Try it for a few minutes. Notice what changes—your breath, your thoughts, your mood. Then do it again tomorrow. You'll start to see that caring for yourself doesn't require a free afternoon or perfect circumstances—just intention.

Sometimes healing starts with five quiet minutes, a deep breath, and a reminder that you deserve your own kindness.

CREATING A GO-TO "CHILL OUT" TOOLKIT FOR MELTDOWNS

Everyone has moments when emotions start spinning out of control—your heart races in class, tears sting at the corners of your eyes, or your hands won't stop shaking during a tough conversation.

You can't always prevent big feelings from showing up, but you *can* prepare for them. That's what a "chill out" Toolkit is: a small collection of things, sounds, and reminders that help bring you back to solid ground when everything feels too much.

Think of it as your personal safety net—a portable calm corner you can carry in your backpack, keep in your nightstand, or store on your phone. When your mind starts to spiral, these items remind you: *You've been here before. You know what to do. You're safe enough to ride this wave.*

This Toolkit isn't about cute accessories for their own sake. It's about meeting yourself with kindness when panic, stress, or sadness threatens to take over. When your brain goes into meltdown mode—at school, at home, in the car—these small tools give you something tangible to hold onto.

***

Grounding Through Touch and Senses

Physical items are often the quickest way to interrupt overwhelm. Something tangible tells your brain, *I'm still here.* Fidget toys, worry stones, or stress balls give your hands something to do and can help slow racing thoughts. Some people carry a smooth pebble from the beach, a tiny piece of fabric, or a coin with texture—objects that feel familiar and grounding.

Scent can be powerful, too. A lightly scented lip balm, essential oil roller, or lavender sachet can instantly shift your body's stress response. (If scents aren't allowed, use texture instead—a soft scrunchie or a bracelet you can twist quietly under your desk.) Even the rhythmic motion of snapping a hair tie against your wrist can discreetly help relieve tension.

***

Digital Comforts That Soothe, Not Overwhelm

Your phone can be part of the problem—but it can also be part of the solution when used intentionally. Create a **"Calm" folder** or album with digital tools that genuinely comfort you. That might include:

A short "comfort playlist" with songs that make you feel safe or steady.

Downloaded meditation or breathing apps for quick grounding (many are free and only a few minutes long).

A photo album filled with happy memories, pets, nature shots, or screenshots of kind messages.

Voice notes from friends or even your own voice saying reassuring things like "You're okay, breathe".

When you're overwhelmed, you won't want to think or search—so make it easy to find these lifelines with one tap.

***

The Power of Words

Sometimes, when the world feels too loud, the right words can become an anchor. Keep a notecard or phone note with calming phrases you can read or whisper to yourself:

> "*I am safe.*"
> "*This will pass.*"
> "*I've handled hard moments before.*"
> Or something funny that makes you smile: "*I survived worse Mondays.*"

You could also jot down a few reminders of things you've overcome—tests you passed, fears you faced, people who care about you. Screenshots of encouraging texts or a short list of affirmations can make a surprising difference in the middle of chaos.

If you tend to freeze when you're upset, include an **emergency contact list**: trusted adults, friends, or helplines you can reach out to without overthinking. Having their names and numbers already written down means you can act rather than panic.

***

Making It Yours

Your Toolkit should fit your life and your environments. If school is a significant stress zone, tuck a few small items in a pencil pouch, makeup bag, or hoodie pocket—something subtle you can grab without drawing attention. For example:

- a small stress ball

- a bracelet or scrunchie you can fidget with quietly

- a sticker or folded note with a calming phrase hidden in your notebook.

At home, create a slightly bigger version: a small box or basket with comforting items—your favorite plush, fuzzy socks, art supplies for doodling, or a journal.

For travel or after-school activities, a "mini version" might live in your phone case or purse: earbuds, gum, or a small crystal or trinket that reminds you of peace.

Many teens also make a **digital calm corner.** They create a phone folder labeled "**Reset**," filled with things that center them: calming playlists, downloaded meditations for when Wi-Fi is weak, or photos that remind them of good days. It's like a pocket-sized sanctuary that moves with you.

***

Real Stories from Real Girls

I've heard from girls who say their toolkits became quiet lifelines in moments they didn't see coming. One student shared how she felt panic rising during an algebra test—her vision blurred, her breathing quickened. She reached for a tiny quartz stone in her pocket and repeated to herself, *"I am okay, just breathe."* It didn't completely erase the panic, but it slowed her enough to finish the test and ask her teacher for help later.

Another girl said she used her comfort playlist after an argument with her mom. She turned off the lights, crawled under her blanket, and let herself cry while her favorite song played. *"It didn't fix everything,"* she said, *"but it helped me feel safe enough to talk again."*

Even when you don't use your Toolkit, just knowing it exists can make meltdowns feel less terrifying. It's proof that you've planned for your own care—that you trust yourself to handle complex emotions when they come.

***

Your Toolkit = Your Power

Building a "chill out" kit isn't about weakness; it's about wisdom. It's an act of foresight—like packing an umbrella because you know storms are part of life. No one gets through without rough days or meltdowns. Having tools ready means you don't have to start from zero every time.

Start small.

Pick one or two things that bring you comfort and build from there. Add new pieces over time and swap out any that stop working. Your needs will change, and that's okay.

Each time you reach for your Toolkit instead of spiraling, you prove something important: you know how to care for yourself. That's not childish—**it's strength.**

***

Red Flags of Burnout — How to Spot It Early and Stop It

Burnout rarely crashes all at once. It creeps up quietly, blending into everyday life until one day you realize you're running on fumes.

At first, it's small things: snapping at people for no reason, zoning out in class, losing excitement for something you used to love. You might tell yourself you're just tired or in a bad mood—but that low-level exhaustion, irritability, and disinterest are often early warning signs that your body and mind are waving a flag for help.

Maybe you find yourself counting the minutes until you can crawl into bed, or feeling annoyed at texts from friends who want to hang out. Perhaps you've stopped laughing at things that usually crack you up, or your favorite hobbies feel like chores.

It's easy to blame stress, hormones, or a "rough week," but if the fog doesn't lift, burnout might be settling in.

***

How to Recognize the Signs

Spotting burnout means paying attention to subtle changes in your usual patterns. Everyone has exhausting days or demanding weeks—finals, games, performances, family drama—but burnout feels different. It sticks around. It drains joy from things that once gave you life. Your concentration dips, your patience thins, and you start going through the motions instead of actually living your days.

> **Here's a quick self-check:**
> - Have I lost interest in things I used to enjoy?
> - Am I more irritable or quicker to snap?
> - Do I feel tired even after plenty of sleep?
> - Am I zoning out, forgetting details, or missing deadlines?
> - Do I feel like I'm surviving each day instead of living it?

If several of these sound like you, it's probably not just a "bad week." Burnout is your mind's way of saying, *something has to give.*

***

Small Steps to Stop the Spiral

The good news: burnout can be reversed when you catch it early. It starts with protecting your energy.

1. Learn to say no

People often slide into burnout because they keep saying yes—to every project, every favor, every "Can you just...?"—until there's nothing left to give. Saying no can feel scary, especially if you hate disappointing people, but you can't pour from an empty cup.

Try a calm, honest line like, *"I'd love to help, but I can't take anything else on right now."*

Boundaries aren't rejection; they're protection.

2. Schedule reset time

Rest doesn't have to be a full day under blankets (though if you can, do it). Even carving out an hour matters. Treat it like a real appointment—no homework, no obligations, no multitasking.

Do something that genuinely soothes you: walk outside, stretch, doodle, watch a comfort show, or lie down and breathe.

If long breaks aren't realistic, build *micro-rests* into your day: a slow walk to class, a deep-breathing pause between assignments, five minutes of music before bed. These short resets signal your nervous system that it's safe to recharge.

3. Ask for help

You don't have to shoulder everything alone. Tell someone what's going on—*"I'm maxed out,"* *"I'm overwhelmed,"* or *"I need a day to catch up."*

Delegating a task or switching chores isn't a weakness; it's teamwork. Let people support you—they can't read your mind, but they'll often step up when you give them the chance.

If you're not sure who to ask for help, consider reaching out to a trusted friend, family member, or school counselor.

***

What Burnout Looks Like in Real Life

For instance, Madi, who loved marching band, noticed she stopped caring about performances and felt numb even after big wins. She dropped one extracurricular for a season and immediately felt lighter and more present.

Aria had been snapping at her family and crying over tiny things. One night, she told her mom she needed a mental-health day. They spent it baking and watching movies, and afterward, she realized how long it had been since she'd laughed freely.

Dani kept forgetting assignments and zoning out. She started using a planner—*not* to cram in more tasks, but to schedule rest the same way she scheduled deadlines. Giving rest a name and time helped her stop feeling guilty for it.

Burnout doesn't look identical for everyone, but it feels the same at its core: dull, heavy, and endless. Naming it is powerful—it turns the fog into something you can walk through instead of getting lost in.

***

The Burnout Check-In

Grab a notebook or open your notes app. Ask yourself:
- What's one thing I've stopped enjoying lately?

- When was the last time I truly relaxed without feeling guilty?

- What's one commitment I could say no to this week?

Write freely and honestly. You might start to see patterns—like certain classes, apps, or relationships that always leave you depleted. Awareness gives you the chance to make minor but meaningful adjustments.

***

Permit Yourself to Pause

Burnout isn't a sign of weakness or failure; it's a sign that you've been trying too hard for too long without refueling. It's your body whispering, *Please slow down before I make you.* The sooner you listen, the easier recovery becomes.

Catching burnout early means you can rest before you collapse, ask for help before you withdraw, and rekindle joy before it fades.

Self-care isn't selfish; it's how you keep your spark alive. Protecting that spark—your curiosity, laughter, and sense of purpose—is the kind of strength that lasts. Remember, taking care of your energy is just as vital as caring for others-maybe even more.

So, don't feel guilty about prioritizing your own well-being. It's not a luxury, it's a necessity.

Before Reflection:

Before you move on, take a slight pause for yourself. A deep breath. A stretch. A reminder that slowing down matters too.

Reflection: Permission to Pause

Rest is not weakness—it's wisdom. When you slow down, you give your mind and heart a chance to catch up with your life. Keep reminding yourself that peace is productive too.

The world moves fast—but your strength grows in stillness.

Chapter 5

Goals, Grit, and Growth Mindset

Leveling Up Your Life (Your Way)

Picture this: you're sitting in health class while the teacher draws yet another "SMART goals" chart on the board. You've seen it before—specific, measurable, achievable, blah, blah, blah. It feels stiff, forced, and completely disconnected from your actual life. No wonder most people sigh, zone out, or doodle in the margins.

***

GOAL-SETTING FOR GIRLS WHO HATE GOAL-SETTING

If goal-setting has ever felt like just another to-do list about grades, weight, or pleasing other people, you're not imagining it. The way adults talk about goals can make them feel like a chore instead of something empowering. But real goals—the kind that spark excitement instead of pressure—don't need fancy acronyms or deadlines. They need to *matter to you*.

***

Flipping the Script on Goals

A lot of girls avoid setting goals because they've been tied to everyone else's expectations. "Get straight A's." "Make varsity." "Be more confident."

But what if we flipped the script? What if goals weren't about who you *should* be, but who you *want* to become—bit by bit, in ways that feel true to your life?

Start small. Think creatively, not perfectly. Instead of intimidating plans like "change my whole morning routine," try "remember my water bottle" or "make my bed three days in a row."

Tiny goals might sound silly, but they're powerful because they give you daily proof that you can follow through. That's what builds grit—not pressure, but consistency.

When goals are small and personal, they stop feeling like assignments and start feeling like *freedom*. You're steering the ship.

Ask yourself:

"What's one thing—big or small—that would make life a little better by Friday?"

Please write it down, text it to yourself, or whisper it to yourself before bed. No grades. No guilt. Just choose something that matters to you.

***

Make It Visual (or Not—You Decide)

If you're a hands-on or visual thinker, make your goals visible. Vision boards aren't just a Pinterest trend—they're a way to remind yourself what you're working toward.

Grab magazines, scissors, tape, and a poster board, or go digital with Canva or Pinterest. Don't like cutting things out? Use sticky notes, washi tape, or even doodles in a notebook.

Or keep it minimal. Habit trackers, sticker charts on a water bottle, or a few daily checkboxes in your planner all work. Every time you see progress—no matter how small—it gives your brain a little dopamine hit that says, *keep going.*

If writing's not your thing, try voice memos.

Record a quick message to your future self: *"Hey, remember when you thought you couldn't finish that project? You did."* Or leave yourself a pep talk before a big day. Listening back later can be surprisingly motivating—it's your own voice reminding you what you're capable of.

***

Goals That Actually Fit Your Life

Goals don't have to sound impressive to count. Sure, raising your math grade is excellent—but so is learning to cook one meal, finally organizing your backpack, or making one new friend.

They can be emotional goals: texting a friend first when you feel anxious, journaling after stressful days, or standing up for yourself in a small way.

They can be creative goals, such as finishing a sketchbook page, writing a short poem, or learning a new song on guitar. They can even be courageous goals: saying hi to someone new, joining a club, or trying something that scares you just a little.

Even "weird" goals count. Want to start a windowsill mini-garden? Teach your dog a trick? Push for better recycling at school?

Those are all real goals—because they reflect who *you* are, not who anyone else expects you to be.

***

How to Stay Motivated Without Burning Out

Success looks different for everyone. Your dream is performing on stage. It could be as simple as getting through a presentation without crying. Both are valid wins. The key is to celebrate them equally.

Instead of asking, *"Am I there yet?"* ask, *"What progress have I made this week?"* Each tiny win—every completed sketch, every brave moment—builds self-trust. And that trust is the root of grit and resilience.

If you fall off track, don't turn it into an all-or-nothing spiral. Missing one day doesn't erase the effort that came before. You're training consistency, not perfection.

Interactive Element: Your "Anti-Boring" Goal Menu

Open your notebook or Notes app. Write three things you could try, finish, or change by next week—no matter how small.

- **Something social:** "Compliment someone I don't know well."

- **Something creative:** "Draw with my eyes closed for five minutes."

- **Something personal:** "Leave my phone in another room during dinner."

Pick the one that feels most doable. Now, choose two ways to track it—habit stickers, daily voice memos, text updates to a friend, or checkboxes in your planner. Want ideas? Look up "vision board for teens" or "habit tracker inspo" online, or ask a friend what helps them stay on track.

The point isn't to do everything. It's to find *one small thing* that feels like movement.

***

Make It Fun Again

One reader told me she started calling her goals "quests" instead—it made her feel like the main character in a game rather than a student checking boxes. Another used doodle charts for her goals; every time she met one, she colored in part of a design. A third used mini-rewards: finishing her homework meant 10 guilt-free minutes of a favorite show. These tiny shifts made her feel proud, not pressured.

You can do the same. Reward your effort, not just the outcome. Even crossing off a sticky note or listening to your "victory song" after completing a small goal reinforces progress.

***

Own the Journey

Remember: your goals don't have to look like anyone else's. They can be quirky, creative, low-key, or ambitious. They can change weekly or last the entire semester. The real win is that they're *yours*.

Setting your own goals—and seeing yourself keep even one small promise—builds a kind of quiet confidence that no grade or trophy ever could. It's how you learn to trust yourself, recover faster when things go wrong, and build a life that actually fits you.

Forget the charts. Forget the pressure. Start with what excites you, what challenges you, and what makes you feel alive.

That's what real goal-setting looks like—and it's so much better than "SMART."

***

THE "FAIL-FORWARD" FORMULA — TURNING MISTAKES INTO FUEL

Failure lands like a slap. It stings, it lingers, and sometimes it makes you want to disappear before anyone notices. You may have studied for a quiz and still bombed it. Maybe you froze during your first solo or missed the winning shot after weeks of practice. That awful mix of embarrassment and regret can feel heavy enough to knock the air out of you. You replay it over and over, wishing you could erase it—or at least shrink it until nobody remembers.

Here's the truth: failing doesn't mean you're not good enough. It doesn't mean you should give up or that you don't belong. Every single person who's ever gotten better at anything—sports, music, art, friendship, activism—has crashed, fumbled, or fallen flat at some point. What separates people who grow from those who stop isn't talent or luck; it's what they do next.

***

What Failing Forward Really Means

A reader once messaged me after her first debate meet. She blanked mid-speech, forgot half her argument, and spent the rest of the round wanting to melt into the floor. Afterward, she hid in the bathroom, convinced she could never show her face again. But a few days later, she signed up for the next debate. *"If I could survive that,"* she told me, *"I can handle anything."*

That's failing forward—turning a mistake into momentum instead of a roadblock. It's the decision to keep showing up, even when your confidence wobbles.

***

Step One: Face It, Don't Flee It

The first step is simply noticing what happened. Most people skip this part because it feels uncomfortable—but it's the foundation of growth. Write down what went wrong as plainly as possible. No excuses, no drama, just facts: *"I mixed up my lines," "I panicked and guessed on half the test,"* or *"I procrastinated until it was too late."*

Then, name the feelings underneath. Are you angry, embarrassed, disappointed, sad, or scared? Naming emotions doesn't make them stronger—it makes them *manageable*. When you say, *"I feel embarrassed,"* your brain starts processing it instead of letting it swirl like fog.

***

Step Two: Normalize It

The next step is to remember that this isn't just *your* failure. Everyone messes up. Every athlete misses crucial shots. Every singer has cracked a note on stage. Every leader has made decisions that didn't go the way they hoped. If you dig into the stories of people you admire, you'll find plenty of rough drafts before the final masterpiece.

If you need proof, look up some of your favorite creators or athletes—many openly share their early mistakes. That's not a coincidence; it's how growth happens. Failure is the tuition fee of experience.

***

Step Three: Get Curious, Not Cruel

Once you've faced what happened and reminded yourself that you're human, ask the golden question: *What can I learn from this?*

> **Instead of spiraling into "I'll always fail," shift toward curiosity. Ask:**
> *"What exactly tripped me up?"*
> *"Was I underprepared, overtired, or distracted?"*
> *"What's one thing I could do differently next time?"*

You may need more rest before tests, to practice out loud instead of in your head, or to ask for help sooner. The point isn't to find someone to blame—it's to collect data about what works for you.

***

Step Four: Make a "Fail-Forward" Worksheet

Grab a notebook and create your own worksheet:

- **Describe what happened.** Keep it factual and short.

- **Name your feelings.** (Even if it's "ugh, everything.")

- **List three lessons.** These can be about the skill *or* about yourself. For example:

  1. *"Skipping breakfast made me more anxious."*

  2. *"Practicing with a friend helped me remember more."*

  3. *"I need to plan smaller goals next time."*

- **End with one next step.** A tiny one—like *"ask a classmate to quiz me," "record myself once,"* or *"take three deep breaths before I start."*

Over time, this list becomes proof that you can recover—and that every mistake makes you a little wiser.

***

A Gentle Reframe

Try this journaling prompt:
"If my best friend failed exactly like I did, what would I say to her?"

You'd probably tell her she did her best, that one test or one performance doesn't define her, that she can try again and improve.

Offer yourself that same compassion. Be the friend you need, not the critic you fear.

***

Stories That Show It Works

One reader bombed her solo but decided to help with costumes for the school musical. That backstage experience reignited her love of performing—she auditioned again the following year, this time with more confidence.

Another didn't make varsity and felt crushed—until she joined a local rec league focused on teamwork rather than competition. *"I remembered why I loved the sport,"* she said.

A third reader failed a math test she'd studied hard for. Instead of giving up, she met with her teacher, learned new study techniques, and later that semester ended up tutoring a friend. *"Helping someone else made me realize I'd actually learned more than I thought,"* she told me.

Each story has the same core: the setback wasn't the end—it was the beginning of a new kind of strength.

***

Choosing to Rise Again

Failing forward doesn't erase disappointment, but it transforms it into something useful. It's choosing to say, *I'm still learning,* instead of *I'll never get this right.*

Every time you show up again—with shaky hands, a bruised ego, or a nervous heart—you're proving something powerful: **resilience grows in the mess, not the spotlight.**

Mistakes aren't the opposite of success—they're part of the process that builds it. When you turn failure into feedback and keep moving, you stop letting it define you. You learn to explain it.

So, take a breath, pick up your notebook, and start again. You're not back at zero—you're already one try stronger than before.

***

CELEBRATING PROGRESS (NOT JUST PERFECTION)

There's a persistent myth that only the big wins count—the A+ on the test, the starting spot on the team, the perfect solo, the acceptance letter.

Somewhere along the way, we learn that effort doesn't matter unless it earns applause. It's easy to start believing that if you're not number one, you're invisible. But here's the truth nobody says out loud: showing up, pushing through awkwardness, or simply *not quitting* often matters more than the trophy moments.

Practicing a new skill for five minutes, even when you're tired, is growth. Studying a little longer than last week is progress. Choosing to get out of bed and try again after a rough night—that's courage in action. Every small step is evidence that you're building something real and resilient.

***

Why Small Wins Matter

Big goals might get the headlines, but it's the small wins that truly build the foundation. They're the quiet moments that strengthen self-belief—the kind that rarely get posted or praised but make all the difference over time. When you track those mini-successes, you start to see yourself differently. Instead of focusing on how far you have to go, you start realizing how far you've already come. These small wins are not just stepping stones; they are the building blocks of your success.

Don't wait for someone else to notice. Celebrate the wins only *you* see:

- speaking up in class when your voice trembles

- finishing an assignment early, even if it's not perfect

- walking into a room that once made you anxious

- choosing to rest rather than overwork when you're exhausted.

Those in-between steps are the real proof of progress—the parts most people skip or rush through.

***

Making Progress Visible

When progress feels invisible, motivation fades. That's why marking it in small, creative ways helps you see what's really happening.

Some girls keep **progress jars**, dropping in a bead, coin, or folded note every time they show up for themselves. Over time, the jar fills and becomes a physical reminder of consistency—proof that growth is happening, even when it's slow.

Others create **"win walls."** Sticky notes, index cards, or tiny affirmations line a wall, mirror, or locker. Each one marks a small victory: *"Spoke in class," "Finished chapter two," "Didn't check my phone before bed."* The effect is powerful—a visual highlight reel of effort, not perfection.

If you're more digital, create a **"Wins" album** on your phone. Snap quick photos, screenshot kind messages, or add short notes whenever something goes well. On hard days, scrolling through those moments can lift your mood more than any pep talk.

***

Turning Progress into Ritual

Celebrating progress works best when it becomes a ritual-something you do often enough that your brain starts associating effort with pride, not pressure.

Some girls blast their favorite playlist and dance for two minutes after finishing a tough assignment. Others treat themselves to a cozy snack, wear fuzzy socks, or send a silly *"I did it!"* selfie to a friend. These personal rituals not only make the celebration more enjoyable, but they also reinforce the value of your *effort and progress*.

One reader told me she used to cry after every soccer practice where she didn't score. Her coach challenged her to start celebrating every time she passed the ball or hustled back on defense. Within weeks, practice became fun again. *"I realized I loved playing, not just scoring,"* she said.

Another girl kept a "proud moments" note on her phone. Each time she handled something difficult—like talking to a teacher about a grade or apologizing after an argument—she added a line. Months later, that note read like a story of quiet courage.

***

Interactive Element: The Progress Jar Ritual

Find an empty jar, mug, or container. This will be your progress jar. Each time you do something that requires effort—practicing your instrument, finishing your homework, reaching out to a friend—drop in a bead, paper slip, or coin.

> **Write short notes like:**
> *"Showed up even when I was nervous."*
> *"Finished the draft."*
> *"Did my best today."*

When the jar starts to fill, please take a moment to look at it. That's what persistence looks like—visible proof that you keep trying. On bad days, pull out a few slips to remind yourself how much progress you've made, even when it didn't feel like much at the time.

***

Learning to Notice the Middle

Progress doesn't always feel exciting. Sometimes it's boring, repetitive, or quiet. That's where real growth happens—between the dramatic before-and-after photos, in the middle of the grind.

Try building a habit of noticing: after each study session, practice, or emotional win, take five seconds to say, *"That counted."* Write it down, whisper it, high-five yourself—whatever fits. That small acknowledgment trains your brain to see effort as worthy in its own right.

***

Progress Over Perfection

Celebrating progress isn't about ignoring mistakes or pretending life's perfect. It's about honoring your effort, consistency, and resilience—especially when no one's watching.

One student once told me, *"I used to think success was the medal at the end. Now I celebrate the days I don't quit."* That's the shift that builds absolute confidence.

So make your own rules for celebration. It could be your favorite show after three study sessions. It could be journaling one good thing from every week. It could be just taking a quiet breath and saying, *I'm proud of me.*

Perfection is a moving target. Progress, on the other hand, is everywhere—you have to notice it.

Each time you honor your effort, you remind yourself that you're building something lasting, one step at a time.

You don't have to wait for the finish line to celebrate. You've already started winning.

CREATING YOUR OWN "GLOW-UP" ROADMAP

Picture this: a page, a screen, or even the back of your notebook becomes your personal space—a safe zone where you can spill ideas, doodles, and goals without judgment. Think of it as a *living map* of who you're becoming: full of hopes, hiccups, and every spark of progress you've made along the way.

This isn't about building a strict plan that boxes you in. It's an evolving guide you design yourself—tracking where you want to grow, what might trip you up, who's in your corner, and one next step that keeps you moving.

> Grab a sheet of paper, your favorite notebook, or open a digital tool like Canva, Notion, or even your Notes app. Divide your page into four sections:
> **Dreams, Obstacles, Support Squad,** and **Next Micro-Step**
> Don't worry about making it perfect—think doodles, color, short phrases, or even magazine clippings that make you feel *something*.

***

1. Dreams—Your Spark List

Start with *dreams*. Write down or draw anything that excites you, no matter how random or far-off it feels. Maybe it's feeling less anxious meeting new people, running a mile without stopping, or finally sharing your poetry online. These aren't just the "acceptable" goals that teachers or adults talk about — they're your *real* wants. They can be messy, funny, or heartfelt.

There's no dream too small or too weird to include.

Try to imagine how each dream would *feel*: the calm of finishing something that used to scare you, the thrill of seeing your art in print, the quiet pride of handling stress a little better than before. When you connect your goals to feelings instead of just results, they become more motivating and personal.

***

2. Obstacles—What Might Get in the Way

Now, move to *obstacles*. Get honest here. What could make this hard? List your worries, time limits, distractions, or inner doubts. Maybe your fear of embarrassment freezes you, or procrastination sneaks in whenever things get uncomfortable. You may compare yourself to others or talk yourself out of trying at all.

This isn't a list of reasons you'll fail—it's a roadmap of *what to prepare for*. When you name what might block your path, you can start planning detours before you get stuck. Every obstacle holds information about how you work, not evidence that you can't.

If it helps, think of each one as a speed bump, not a stop sign. Write next to each obstacle one tiny strategy that could help: *"Ask for help when I get stuck," "Set a timer for ten minutes,"* or *"Remind myself that everyone starts somewhere."* These small ideas turn barriers into part of the plan instead of something to fear.

***

3. Support Squad—Who's in Your Corner

Next up: *your support squad.* Who cheers you on? This could be anyone—your best friend who texts *"You got this,"* a teacher who listens without judgment, a sibling who cracks jokes to break tension, or even an online creator whose videos make you feel seen.

And yes, include yourself. You might be the quiet backbone of your own success—the one who keeps trying even when nobody notices.

Write their names, draw symbols, or add photos or emojis if you're digital. If you like visuals, create a mini collage of people, quotes, or affirmations that remind you you're not alone. Seeing your support system laid out reminds you that growth is a *team effort,* even if some of the team sends memes at midnight.

***

4. The Next Micro-Step—Tiny Moves, Real Progress

This part is where your map comes alive. Under *Next Micro-Step*, pick one small action that nudges you forward. Make it so simple that it almost feels too easy.

If you dream of feeling stronger in gym class, your micro-step could be putting your sneakers by the door tonight.

If your goal is to speak up more, write one affirmation on a sticky note—*"My voice matters"*—and place it on your mirror.

If you dream of writing a story, open a document and type the title. That's it.

Micro-steps might look small, but they carry serious power. They train your brain to connect effort with satisfaction instead of fear. Each time you complete one, you prove to yourself that progress doesn't need to be dramatic to count.

***

Design It Your Way

Make your roadmap *feel like you.* Use highlighters, gel pens, stickers, or washi tape. Add glitter, pressed flowers, or doodles. If you're using Canva or Notion, customize the colors, fonts, or backgrounds that lift your mood. If you're not into words every day, use symbols—a star for progress, a wave for resilience, a heart for moments of kindness.

Your roadmap should energize you when you look at it, not feel like homework.

***

Check-In Moments

Set monthly checkpoints to look back and ask:

- What's working right now?

- Where did I get stuck?

- What surprised me this month?

- What tiny win am I proud of?

Use prompts like *"Biggest glow-up moment," "Something I learned,"* or *"One thing I'll try next."*

Maybe you auditioned and didn't make the team—but you still showed up. Perhaps you helped a friend through a rough night and realized you're a good listener. Reflection turns your journey into something you can actually *see*.

***

Stories from the Map

One girl I know wanted to start a mental health club at school. She ran into paperwork, pushback, and weeks of waiting—but she kept going, gathered allies, and eventually got the club approved. Another realized she no longer loved being first chair in orchestra and switched to learning guitar on YouTube. *"It felt like rediscovering my joy,"* she said.

Others track non-academic glow-ups: one girl drew a star on her wrist every time she spoke up in class. By the end of the semester, her arm looked like a galaxy—and she finally saw how much she'd grown.

***

Keep It Flexible

Let your roadmap shift as you do. If a dream stops fitting, replace it. If an obstacle fades, erase it. Add new people to your support squad as your world expands—swap micro-steps when your goals evolve. Flexibility isn't failure—it's proof you're paying attention to your own growth.

What makes this roadmap powerful is ownership. No one else defines what success or "glow-up" means for you. Every scribble, sticker, and edit is a record of how far you've come.

Life moves, and so will your map. Some weeks, you'll sprint; others, you'll crawl—**both count.**

The magic is in returning to the map, again and again, even when progress feels invisible.

Because every small reflection, every shift, every note you add is one more step toward the person you're becoming.

Before Reflection:

You've learned a lot about progress and persistence. Before you set your next goal, take a second to recognize how far you've come.

Reflection: Growth in Motion

Progress isn't always visible—but it's happening. Every step, every setback, every try-again moment is part of your growth. Keep moving forward, even if it's one small choice at a time. You're building something more substantial than perfection: **resilience.**

You are the proof that growth is not about speed—it's about courage to begin again.

Chapter 6

Being Seen & Making a Difference

Advocacy, Friendship, and Owning Your Voice

Picture this: it's late, and you're scrolling through messages, wondering if the group making plans actually thought to include you. Maybe someone who hardly ever texts leaves a casual comment on your post, and it makes you pause. You wonder: *if things got hard, would these people really have my back?* That's when the difference between a true friend and a "follower" becomes crystal clear.

***

HOW TO SPOT AND BE A TRUE FRIEND (NOT JUST A "FOLLOWER")

A true friend is more than a spectator. She notices when your energy shifts, asks if you're okay, and remembers the small, specific things—your favorite playlist before exams, how you like your coffee, the jokes that always make you laugh. She checks in because she cares, not because it's convenient. She celebrates your wins, respects your space, and doesn't disappear when things get messy.

By contrast, surface-level acquaintances tend to drift in and out depending on what they can get from you. They might show up when things are fun or easy, but fade away when life turns heavy. Followers see your *highlight reel* online; true friends see the behind-the-scenes you—the unfiltered version who's sometimes tired, confused, or just quiet.

***

How to Recognize Real Friendship

Checking in on your friendships can feel awkward, but it's one of the most powerful things you can do for your emotional health. It's a moment of self-reflection that can lead to a deeper understanding of your relationships. This self-reflection empowers you to take control of your relationships and ensure they are healthy and supportive. Ask yourself honestly:

- Does this friend celebrate my wins or compete with me?

- Can I trust her with my secrets?

- Does she respect my boundaries when I say "no"?

- Does she show up when I'm struggling, or only when things are fun?

- Do I feel more myself—or more drained—after hanging out?

If you find yourself answering "no" to most of these, it's worth reflecting on it. Friendships can drift or shift over time, and not every connection is meant to last forever. What matters most is whether the relationship adds *support* to your life or *stress.*

Healthy friendships are about balance: both parties listen, both give and receive, and both apologize when they make mistakes. It's normal for one person to need more care at times—but over time, it should even out.

What Real Support Looks Like

Being a strong friend isn't about dramatic gestures or perfectly timed advice. Most of the time, it's about showing up in small, thoughtful ways—sending a "good luck" text before a test, remembering a birthday with a doodle or a meme, and sitting next to someone who looks nervous—checking in after a tough day.

Those little things add up—they build safety and trust. Real friends hold space for each other's feelings instead of rushing to fix them. When a friend is hurting, you don't have to have the perfect words; sometimes just saying, *"I'm here, and I care,"* is enough.

***

Friendship Reflection

Try this quick reflection:

Write down one friend who leaves you feeling calm and seen—and one who often leaves you tense, anxious, or unsure.

What makes the difference between them? Look for patterns: honesty, laughter, kindness, reliability. The more aware you become of what *healthy* feels like, the easier it gets to protect your peace.

Here's a simple **Friendship Health Check** to use anytime things feel off:
- Do they celebrate my wins without jealousy?

- Do they keep my private thoughts private?

- Can I say no without guilt?

- Do they ask how I'm really doing?

- Is the friendship balanced most of the time?

- Can I be my whole self around them?

If most answers are yes, nurture that friendship—it's gold. If most are no, it might be time for a boundary or even a quiet goodbye.

***

When Friendships Change

Even great friendships can shift. Sometimes life moves people in different directions—different schools, new interests, or changing priorities. That doesn't mean it failed. It means it *evolved*.

You can be grateful for what the friendship was while accepting that it might not fit forever.

And then there are times when a friendship crosses a line: repeated gossip, broken trust, constant negativity. If that happens, you have every right to step back. It's a powerful act of self-respect and self-care. Letting go isn't betrayal—it's self-respect.

One girl told me her best friend began sharing her private messages as jokes in group chats. It took weeks of confusion and hurt before she confronted her, saying, *"That broke my trust, and I need space."* It wasn't easy, but afterward, she said, *"For the first time, I felt free."*

***

Being the Friend You Want to Have

If you want better friendships, start by being that kind of friend yourself.

Practice listening without interrupting. Ask how someone really feels instead of assuming. Respect their boundaries even if you don't always understand them. Be honest and kind, not perfect.

This encouragement inspires you to be the best friend you can be, which in turn improves your relationships.

Standing up for friends who are being excluded can change everything. If you notice someone being left out, send an invite, share a seat, or start a conversation. You might be the only person who does—and that small act can build trust faster than any long speech.

One reader told me she sat with a new student at lunch after noticing that no one else did. That one lunch turned into a friendship that lasted years. *"I almost didn't go over,"* she said, *"but I'm so glad I did."* It's a testament to the transformative power of small acts of kindness in building trust and connection.

***

Redefining Friendship in the Social Media Era

In a world that measures connection in likes and followers, friendship can feel like a popularity contest. But popularity isn't the same as belonging. Belonging feels quiet, steady, and safe. It's laughter you don't have to force, conversations you don't have to edit, and trust you don't have to question.

You don't need hundreds of people to feel supported—just a few who see you clearly and care about the real you.

***

The Bigger Picture

Friendship isn't one big thing; it's a thousand small, consistent actions—honesty, loyalty, showing up when it's inconvenient, forgiving when it's hard. When you focus less on collecting followers and more on *building connections,* you'll find relationships that last and lift you.

Be the kind of friend you needed on your hardest day, and you'll attract others who do the same.

That's how real friendships begin—and how they endure.

***

ADVOCACY 101 — STANDING UP FOR YOURSELF AND OTHERS

Advocacy is about using your voice—not just to get what *you* need, but to help people who might not feel able to speak up.

A lot of people imagine advocacy as megaphones, protests, or fiery TV speeches. But most of the time, it looks quieter and more personal. It's the moments when you say, "This matters," whether the issue is yours or someone else's.

It might be asking for extra help in math, even though you're nervous, someone will think you're not smart enough. It could be noticing when a classmate is left out and choosing to speak up. It might even be gently correcting a friend who misgenders someone, knowing it could feel uncomfortable but right.

Advocacy can seem intimidating, but at its heart, it's just about showing up—for yourself, for others, and for what you believe in.

***

Starting Small

If you're not used to putting your needs first, asking for something can feel awkward or selfish. But it's not. Self-advocacy is simply recognizing that your voice has worth. And you don't have to start with confrontation or conflict.

Start tiny. Send an email to a teacher that says, *"Hi, I'm confused about this assignment—could we find a time to review it?"* Or pause at the lunch table and invite someone who's been sitting alone: *"Hey, want to join us?"*

These small actions train your brain to see that speaking up makes a difference. Each time you use your voice, even in a whisper, you remind yourself—and others—that you deserve to be heard.

One student told me she practiced advocacy by emailing her teacher every Friday about one thing she didn't understand that week. *"At first, I felt embarrassed,"* she said. *"Then I realized it wasn't awkward anymore—it was just being honest."*

That's advocacy: small, repeated acts of honesty that create change.

When Something Feels Unfair

It could be a club that includes only a particular group. Grading may feel inconsistent, or you notice someone being treated differently. Advocacy can look like calmly naming what you see and asking how it can improve.

You might say:

"I noticed that only certain students get to participate. Could we make it more inclusive?"

"This rule feels unfair—can we talk about how it's applied?"

You don't have to be confrontational to be powerful. A calm tone, clear words, and respectful curiosity often open more doors than anger or silence.

***

Scripts for Speaking Up

When you're nervous, it helps to have words ready. Try these starters:

> *"I'd like to talk about something that's been making me uncomfortable."*
> *"Can we discuss something I've noticed?"*
> *"I saw ___ happen, and it didn't sit right with me. What can we do about it?"*
> *"I work best with extra time on assignments because of my learning needs. Is that possible?"*

These phrases are minor keys—they unlock conversations without slamming doors. Some people will listen right away; others might not get it at first. That doesn't mean your concern isn't valid.

Remember: you can always follow up later, write instead of speaking, or bring in an ally if the situation feels intimidating. The goal isn't to win every time—it's to stay true to your values.

***

Real Stories of Courage

Real change often begins when one person decides silence isn't an option.

One student noticed her school had no gender-inclusive bathrooms. For weeks, she went back and forth about whether to say something. *"I didn't want to be the 'problem student,"* she said.

Finally, she started a petition and brought it to the principal. Some students rolled their eyes. Others thanked her quietly in the hallway. It took months, but the school added an inclusive bathroom.

Another student noticed a classmate being misgendered by teachers. At first, she only comforted her friend privately. Eventually, she started gently correcting people: *"Actually, they use they/them pronouns."* Her voice shook at first. But each correction made the next one easier. Within weeks, other classmates followed her lead—and respectful language became the norm.

Neither of these girls shouted or demanded attention. They spoke up calmly, consistently, and with heart—and that made the difference.

***

Self-Advocacy Counts, Too

Advocacy isn't always about fixing entire systems; it's often about improving your own experience.

One girl with a reading disability felt embarrassed asking for help. After months of struggling silently, she emailed her English teacher: *"I need extra time on quizzes. Is there a way to make that happen?"* The teacher responded kindly and helped her set up an accommodation plan.

That single message changed her whole school year—and gave her more confidence for every conversation afterward.

Each time you advocate for yourself, you set an example for others who might be watching. You show them it's possible.

***

Building the Muscle

If the idea of speaking up makes your heart race, you're far from alone. Most people—adults included—get nervous about rocking the boat. Especially girls who've been taught to be "easygoing" or "polite." But courage doesn't mean never being scared—it means caring enough to act *even though* you're afraid.

Advocacy is like a muscle: the more you use it, the stronger it gets. You don't have to change the world overnight. Just start with one small, brave moment. Ask for help. Correct a small injustice. Stand next to someone who's standing alone.

With every quiet step, you're proving that your voice is worth hearing.

***

Reflection Prompt: My Advocacy Starter List

In your journal, write down:

- *One small thing I could speak up about for myself this week.*

- *One way is to support someone else who might need an ally.*

- *One fear I have about using my voice—and one truth that challenges it.*

Even writing these down counts as advocacy—it's the start of awareness.

***

Why This Matters

Advocacy doesn't always sound loud. Sometimes it's a shaky voice in a quiet room. Sometimes it's an email sent after weeks of hesitation. Sometimes it's a simple, steady *no* when everyone expects a *yes*.

But every time you choose truth over silence, you make the world a little fairer—not just for you, but for the next person who finds courage in your example. Your voice doesn't have to be perfect to be powerful. It just has to be yours.

***

Using Your Voice — Speaking Up in Class, Clubs, or Online

You know that feeling: your heart races, your palms sweat, and every part of you wants to melt into your chair instead of raising your hand. It's like your body is shouting, *"Not me!"* That fear is real—a mix of stage fright, fear of being judged, and the tiny whisper of imposter syndrome telling you that you're not intelligent or interesting enough to speak up.

Even when you *know* the answer or have something important to say, your brain plays out the worst-case scenario: *What if I sound dumb? What if nobody cares?* You glance around and imagine everyone watching, waiting for you to mess up.

But here's the truth: most people in the room are thinking about themselves, not about you. Still, knowing that doesn't always quiet the butterflies in your stomach.

I've heard girls say, *"My hands were shaking, but I did it anyway."* That moment—the one where your voice trembles but you speak anyway—is often the beginning of confidence.

***

Start Small, Speak Steady

Finding your voice doesn't mean diving straight into speeches or debates. It starts with something small and doable. You could share one thought in a small group before speaking to the whole class. Or, in a club meeting, volunteer to summarize a point.

Practice in low-pressure settings. Try saying your ideas out loud to your bedroom mirror, your notes app, or even your pet. It might feel silly, but hearing your own words builds familiarity and reduces fear.

Before speaking, try a quick "power pose": stand tall, shoulders back, feet grounded. It's not magic—but it reminds your body that you belong in that space. If your mind tends to go blank, jot a few bullet points on a sticky note or index card. That tiny plan can anchor you when nerves hit.

Confidence doesn't arrive all at once; it grows from small, brave acts, one at a time.

***

What Real Leadership Looks Like

Using your voice isn't about being the loudest person in the room. Some people dominate every discussion and call that leadership, but authentic leadership starts with *listening.*

Notice who hasn't spoken yet and invite them in. Ask, *"What do you think?"* or *"Can you tell me more about your idea?"*

Follow up with curiosity—*"I hadn't thought of it that way; what made you see it like that?"*—to show genuine respect.

That kind of engagement builds trust and draws out new perspectives that would otherwise stay hidden.

Speaking up isn't about spotlighting yourself—it's about creating space where everyone feels safe to share.

***

The Ripple Effect of One Voice

Girls are changing their schools every day just by using their voices. Sometimes it's bold and public; other times, it's quiet and steady.

One student noticed that no one talked about anxiety in her health class, even though half the room admitted privately that they felt it. One day, she raised her hand and said, *"I think we should talk more about what anxiety actually feels like."*

Her voice cracked at first, but classmates nodded. The conversation opened up. By the end of class, several people had shared stories they'd been holding inside—and even the teacher thanked her for starting something real.

That one moment—a single sentence—shifted the whole atmosphere.

***

Your Voice Online

The digital world gives you another powerful way to speak up. You don't have to be an influencer or have thousands of followers to make a difference. Sharing an honest story, posting about a cause you care about, or creating art that reflects your truth can reach people you'll never meet.

You might post a short video about kindness, share a quote that helped you through anxiety, or comment *"I feel this too"* on someone's vulnerable post. Even one small piece of empathy can ripple far.

Online advocacy works best when it's authentic. Post what you *genuinely* believe in, not what you think will get attention. Small, thoughtful content—like encouraging classmates before exams or highlighting local volunteer opportunities—often means more than big, viral posts.

Handling the Harder Moments

Using your voice also means bravely speaking up when something feels off. In a group project, if someone repeats a stereotype or shuts down another person's idea, you can courageously say:

> *"I see it differently."*
> *"I think there's more to consider here."*
> *"That comment didn't sit right with me—can we rephrase that?"*

You might not win everyone over, and not every moment will go smoothly. But respectful honesty earns quiet respect—even from people who disagree right away.

Remember: you don't have to be perfect. Sometimes your words will come out wrong.

Sometimes you'll blush or stammer. That's okay. You spoke up—and that's what matters most.

***

Micro-Challenges to Build Confidence

Confidence grows like a muscle—small reps, over time. Try one "voice challenge" a week:

> *Answer one question in class.*
>
> *Compliment a teammate's idea out loud.*
>
> *Leave a kind, thoughtful comment online.*
>
> *Ask for clarification instead of pretending you understand.*

Each moment teaches your brain, ***I can do this.***

One student told me she set a goal to speak once in every class each week. *"At first,"* she said, *"it felt like jumping into icy water. Now it's just part of my day."*

That's what growth feels like—still a little scary, but so much more possible than before. This is a testament to your resilience and determination.

***

Your Words Plant Seeds

If finding your voice feels hard, remember: every activist, leader, and advocate you admire started the same way—with shaky words, sweaty hands, and a racing heart. They learned by trying, failing, and trying again.

You don't need to wait until you feel fearless to speak. Courage doesn't come first; it follows action. Each time you open your mouth, even if your voice shakes, you plant a seed of confidence in yourself—and sometimes in others, too.

That one brave thing you say today might be the exact thing someone else needed to hear.

BUILDING A PERSONAL SUPPORT SQUAD FOR EVERY SEASON

Support isn't just one best friend or a single go-to person—it's a *constellation* of people, each shining differently depending on what you need.

Your "support squad" might include old friends, new classmates, family members, teachers, coaches, mentors, or even people you've met online who share your interests.

Everyone plays a unique role: a science teacher for academic help, a cousin when you're feeling left out, a coach for encouragement, or someone online who understands a topic that's hard to talk about at home.

When life feels messy or uncertain, that network can become a safety net—a reminder that you're not alone and that help can come from more than one direction. This is a testament to the security and care your support network provides.

***

Map Your Support System

If you've never mapped your network, try this simple exercise. Draw yourself in the center of a page and add circles around you for the people you trust—family, friends, teachers, mentors, classmates, or supportive online contacts. Use lines, doodles, or stickers to show how close you feel to each person. Maybe you can add hearts for people you talk to often and stars for those who give great advice.

Over time, this map will shift. Some connections will fade; others will glow brighter when you need them most. Empty spaces on your map aren't failures—they're invitations to reach outward. Every new stage of life —from a new semester to a big move —is a chance to build fresh circles of support.

Keeping Connections Alive

Building and maintaining your squad matters, especially during transitions. Moving schools or starting a new activity can feel like hitting "reset," but your old connections don't have to disappear.

A quick message to an old teacher —*"Hi! I just wanted to thank you for all the help last year."* — can reignite a meaningful bond.

If you left behind a club or team that made you feel at home, look for a similar group in your new environment—familiar rhythms can anchor you there.

Clubs, youth groups, volunteer projects, and local events are great places to meet people who share your interests. You might find your next mentor at a community garden, a robotics team, or a local art workshop.

Remember: belonging often starts with showing up—once, then again.

***

The Power of Small Gestures

Even when things feel calm, check in with your people. Support grows strongest in ordinary moments, not just during crises. Send a *"Thanks for listening last week"* text, comment encouragement on a friend's post, or drop a short *"Miss you—let's catch up"* message.

Try keeping a mini gratitude list in your phone: jot down names of people who've shown up for you recently. Glancing at that list on a rough day can remind you how much care already surrounds you.

Small, steady gestures—remembering birthdays, checking in after exams, or sending a silly meme—can keep relationships warm. Friendship and mentorship thrive on consistency more than intensity.

Support in Unexpected Places

Support sometimes comes from unexpected directions. During lockdowns, many girls found comfort in online communities: study-buddy Discord groups, pen-pal programs, fandom circles, or moderated mental-health forums. Those digital friendships—when handled safely—became lifelines.

One girl told me she emailed her old basketball coach for a college recommendation. What started as a quick favor turned into a long-distance mentorship and regular check-ins. *"It reminded me that people don't stop caring just because you're not around every day,"* she said.

Online spaces can offer powerful connections, but safety always comes first. Share only what you're comfortable with, keep personal info private, and trust your instincts. When an online space feels supportive and kind, it can become a genuine part of your constellation.

***

Let It Evolve

Your squad will change as you grow—and that's healthy. You might lean on one person for study help, another for late-night venting, and a different one when you need motivation. Some relationships will fade, while others will blossom.

Ask yourself now and then:

- *Who helps me feel seen and grounded?*

- *Who challenges me to grow kindly?*

- *Is there someone I want to reconnect with?*

If you notice a gap, don't panic. Think of it as space for someone new. Sometimes, the next meaningful person in your life is waiting in a class, a club, or even at the other end of a brave hello.

Reaching out takes courage, but it's one of the most life-changing skills you can build. Each new connection you nurture expands your resilience.

***

Quality Over Quantity

A strong support squad isn't about numbers—it's about trust, variety, and balance. You don't need dozens of close friends to feel secure. A few dependable people—each offering something different—are more valuable than a crowd that doesn't really know you.

If one person can't help, someone else usually can. That's the beauty of a constellation: even when one star dims, others still light the sky. You were never meant to carry everything on your own.

My Constellation of Support

> **Grab a journal or open a blank note and write:**
> *"Who are three people I can reach out to when I need help or encouragement?"*
> *"Who helps me laugh or reset when I'm stressed?"*
> *"Who challenges me kindly to be better?"*

If a category feels empty, that's your cue to reach out—to join a new group, start a conversation, or ask for help.

Before Reflection:

Pause here to notice the impact you already make—through your kindness, your voice, your everyday courage.

Reflection: You Make a Difference

Your voice matters more than you know. Every act of kindness, every time you stand up for something true, you leave ripples that reach farther than you can see. You don't need to change the whole world to make it better—you need to show up as you.

Shine quietly, love boldly, and let your light ripple beyond what you can see.

***

Closing Thought

Thriving as a teen depends on connection: building it on purpose, tending it with gratitude, and letting it change as you do.

Your support squad is your anchor through every season—friends who remind you of your worth, mentors who see your potential, and safe spaces that make you feel at home.

Remember, being seen starts with surrounding yourself with people who lift you higher.

Conclusion

Before you set this book down, take a moment to breathe it in:

You've done so much more than just read—**you've *grown.***

You've learned to speak up, to listen to your inner voice, and to protect the space where your peace lives.

You've faced the messy, complicated parts of growing up—the conversations that made your hands shake, the boundaries that felt hard to draw, the days when courage looked like simply showing up anyway. Through all of it, you've learned something essential: **your voice matters.**

You've seen that standing up for yourself doesn't make you mean—it makes you honest.

That setting limits doesn't push people away—it helps the right ones stay close.

That self-care isn't selfish—it's strength in motion.

And that purpose isn't a single moment of clarity—it's built through the small, brave choices you make every day.

Look at what you've built:

• confidence rooted in kindness, not comparison

• friendships that grow through honesty and respect

• resilience to bounce back when things fall apart

• and a sense of purpose that begins and ends with being true to who you are.

Life will keep changing—new schools, new people, new challenges—but you have everything you need to meet it with steady strength. When the noise of the world gets too loud, return to these pages, to your own notes, or to that voice inside that now whispers instead of shouts: *I've got this.*

You don't need to have it all figured out. You need to keep showing up—with curiosity, with courage, and with compassion for yourself and others.

And as you move forward, remember: you have the power to shape the spaces you enter.

Be the friend who listens, the leader who includes, the person who makes others feel safe to be themselves. That's what real influence looks like—it starts small and spreads wide.

Here's your final challenge:

Keep living like you mean it. Keep asking questions. Keep creating spaces where honesty and kindness win.

And when in doubt, come back to what you've learned here—your voice, your values, your vision for who you want to be.

Because you are not just growing up—you're *becoming.*

And that story is still unfolding, one brave page at a time.

Stand tall. Speak truth. Lead with heart.

And never forget: **you are enough, you are capable, and you are exactly where you need to be.**

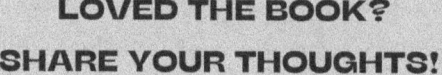

LOVED THE BOOK?
SHARE YOUR THOUGHTS!

Your review means the world! ⭐ It helps other readers discover Teen Girl's Handbook and reminds us that these stories truly make a difference. Thank you for taking a moment to share your honest feedback – every word matters. 💕

📱 Click the link below or scan the QR code
to leave your review on Amazon!

Scan the QR code to leave your review on Amazon!

THANK YOU!

References

Talking With Your Child About Being Left Out
https://www.psychologytoday.com/us/blog/alone-together/202305/talking-with-your-child-about-being-left-out

Chapter 4: Social Media and Friendships
https://www.pewresearch.org/internet/2015/08/06/chapter-4-social-media-and-friendships/

The Influence of Social Exclusion on High School Students ...
https://pmc.ncbi.nlm.nih.gov/articles/PMC10676663/

100 Journaling Prompts for Self-esteem and Confidence
https://www.trishblackwell.com/442-100-journaling-prompts-and-questions-to-boost-your-self-esteem-and-confidence/

How to Help Your Teen Manage Toxic Friendships
https://www.newportacademy.com/resources/empowering-teens/teen-toxic-friendships/

When Your Daughter Isn't Invited, Why Being Excluded Hurts
https://www.thebravegirlproject.com/blog/why-being-excluded-hurts-parent-strategies-for-supporting-teens

Teens, Social Media and Mental Health
https://www.pewresearch.org/internet/2025/04/22/teens-social-media-and-mental-health/

A Teen's Guide to Setting Healthy Boundaries in Friendships
https://www.kidstuffcounseling.com/2024/02/20/a-teens-guide-to-setti
ng-healthy-boundaries-in-friendships/

Exploring the effect of social media on teen girls' mental ...
https://hsph.harvard.edu/news/exploring-the-effect-of-social-media-on-
teen-girls-mental-health/

Empowering Your Feed: The Art Of Deliberate Social ...
https://www.forbes.com/sites/forbeseq/2024/02/23/empowering-your-fe
ed-the-art-of-deliberate-social-media-curation/

Preventing Cyberbullying: Top Ten Tips for Teens
https://cyberbullying.org/preventing-cyberbullying-top-ten-tips-for-teen
s#:~:text=NEVER%20OPEN%20UNIDENTIFIED%20OR%20UNSOLICITED
,Delete%20them%20without%20reading.

Digital Detox and Well-Being | Pediatrics
https://publications.aap.org/pediatrics/article/154/4/e2024066142/199412
/Digital-Detox-and-Well-Being

Why Does My Teen Procrastinate?
https://www.psychologytoday.com/us/blog/emotionally-healthy-teens/2
02006/why-does-my-teen-procrastinate

Test Anxiety Strategies and Study Tips for Kids
https://childmind.org/article/tips-for-beating-test-anxiety/

How to help children and teens manage their stress
https://www.apa.org/topics/children/stress

Balancing School and Social Life: 3 Tips for Teen Girls
https://rootsrenewalranch.com/balancing-academics-and-social-life-tips
-for-girls-to-balance-school-responsibilities-with-social-activities/

The Science of Micro-Wins: How Small Daily Achievements ...
https://ahead-app.com/blog/confidence/the-science-of-micro-wins-how-sm
all-daily-achievements-rewire-your-brain-for-confidence-20250106-204735

How Teens Can Practice Reframing Negative Thoughts
https://www.newportacademy.com/resources/mental-health/reframing-nega
tive-thoughts/

Why GenZs and Millennials are all about 'Main character ...
https://www.harpersbazaar.in/culture/story/why-genzs-and-millennials-are-
all-about-main-character-energyand-heres-how-to-channel-yours-565375-2
023-03-26

Self-compassion: pre-teens and teenagers
https://raisingchildren.net.au/teens/mental-health-physical-health/about-m
ental-health/self-compassion-teenagers

Body image in childhood
https://www.mentalhealth.org.uk/explore-mental-health/articles/body-imag
e-report-executive-summary/body-image-childhood

Snapchat filters changing young women's attitudes - PMC
https://pmc.ncbi.nlm.nih.gov/articles/PMC9577667/

13 Body Positive Instagram Accounts That Make Teens ...
https://grownandflown.com/13-body-positive-instagram-accounts-teens-feel
-great/

Self-Esteem Worksheets for Teens
https://www.therapistaid.com/therapy-worksheets/self-esteem/adolescents

How Anxiety Affects Teenagers
https://childmind.org/article/signs-of-anxiety-in-teenagers/

How to Talk About Mental Health - Young People
https://www.samhsa.gov/mental-health/what-is-mental-health/how-to-talk
/young-people

Real   Stories   On   Mental   Health   From   Young   People
https://www.youngminds.org.uk/young-person/blog/

99   HEALTHY   COPING   SKILLS
https://www.akronchildrens.org/files/99-Healthy-Coping-Skills.html

Social   Belonging   and   Confidence
https://mhanational.org/resources/social-belonging-and-confidence/

Navigating   Cultural   and   Spiritual   Identity   in   Multi-   ...
https://danieldashnawcouplestherapy.com/blog/navigating-cultural-and-spiritual-identity-in-teens

Resource Center https://www.thetrevorproject.org/resources/

5 Safe   Online   Communities   for   Teens   That   Parents   Can   Trust
https://www.brightcanary.io/online-communities-for-teens/

Assertiveness (for Teens) https://kidshealth.org/en/teens/assertive.html

Helping   your   teen   set   boundaries
https://www.loveisrespect.org/resources/helping-your-teen-set-boundaries/

Difficult   conversations   with   pre-teens   and   teenagers
https://raisingchildren.net.au/teens/communicating-relationships/tough-topics/difficult-conversations-with-teens

How   To   Help   Kids   Navigate   BFFs   and   Conflict
https://lindastade.com/teenage-arguments-with-friends/

Diet,   Sleep,   and   Mental   Health: Insights   from   the   UK   ...
https://pmc.ncbi.nlm.nih.gov/articles/PMC8398967/

11 Self Care Ideas for Teens https://www.talkspace.com/blog/self-care-for-teens/

Creating   Your   Own   Adjustable   Self-Care   Toolkit
https://foundrybc.ca/stories/self-care-toolkit/

8 Symptoms   of   Teen   Burnout   and   How   to   Prevent   It
https://www.newportacademy.com/resources/mental-health/teen-burnout/

How   to   Teach   Growth   Mindset   to   Teens
https://biglifejournal.com/blogs/blog/teaching-teens-growth-mindset?srsltid
=AfmBOop-gsYkoUwu_w28aMNkG8LXOdaKxJxkfEVnVFevTnGVfpmSJSVu

Failing   Forward: 7   Stories   of   Success   Through   Failure
https://breakingmuscle.com/failing-forward-7-stories-of-success-through-fai
lure/

How   to   Help   Teens   Set   Effective   Goals   (Tips   &   Templates)
https://biglifejournal.com/blogs/blog/guide-effective-goal-setting-teens-tem
plate-worksheet?srsltid=AfmBOopyHoNIqqWdzX6xGmpm4dNyHcoltzC-ZF
Wi-_12eebpDAU1j_GA

Celebrating   Progress,   Not   Perfection: A   Guide   for   Parents   of   ...
https://www.genieeduhub.com/post/celebrating-progress-not-perfection-a-g
uide-for-parents-of-teens

What   to   Look   for   in   Friendships: Pre-Adolescents   and   Teens
https://evolvetreatment.com/blog/tween-friendships/

Self-advocacy: helping   teenagers   speak   up   for   themselves
https://raisingchildren.net.au/teens/development/social-emotional-develop
ment/self-advocacy-helping-teenagers-speak-up-for-themselves

Speaking   up   changes   everything
https://confidentteens.co.uk/speaking-up-changes-everything/

Kids,   Teens,   and   Young   Adults
https://www.nami.org/kids-teens-and-young-adults/